Dark Psychology Secrets

The Ultimate Guide to Improve Social Influence, Analyze People Using NLP & Body Language Techniques, including tips for Mind Control, Persuasion & Manipulation

Daniel Travis

~ In almost every act of our daily lives, whether in the sphere of politics or business, in our social conduct or our ethical thinking, we are dominated by the relatively small number of persons...who understand the mental processes and social patterns of the masses. It is they who pull the wires which control the public mind. ~
Edward Bernays PROPAGANDA

Copyright © 2019

- Daniel Travis -

Table of Content

Introduction

Congratulations on downloading *Dark Psychology Secrets: The Ultimate Guide to Improve Social Influence, Analyze People Using NLP & Body Language Techniques, including tips for Mind Control, Persuasion & Manipulation* and thank you for doing so.

The following chapters will discuss how and where you encounter the Dark Psychology in your daily life and the kind of people that use these dark techniques to their advantage. Information on Dark Continuum and Dark Singularity will help you understand that Dark Psychology is manifested on a spectrum and all human beings that exist today or have ever existed possess a reservoir of malevolence. The importance and application of evergreen Darwinian theory of "survival of the fittest" and how some of us are genetically inclined to exhibit Dark Psychology more than others.

We will take a trip back to history and study the impact of some major historical events that have left an everlasting impact on the Dark Psychology of humans. A study of human behavioral patterns and their alignment with Dark Psychology to provide you with the ability to successfully decipher these patterns.

In the chapter titled "The Dark Triad", we will deep dive into the dark personality traits of the unholy trinity of Narcissism, Machiavellianism and Psychopathy. You will learn when and how the self love can transition into Narcissism and self harming tendencies. A virtual trip to ancient Italy and meet with philosopher Niccolò Machiavelli, whose proposed tactics and practices of powerful leader gave birth to dictators like Adolf Hitler and Joseph Stalin. You will get to know the Psychopathic Test score of notorious serial killer, Ted Bundy.

Surprising revelations on Neuro-Linguistic programming and how you may be programmed to think and act specifically in response to a particular trigger. You will learn how people can create "anchors" on your body to condition your thoughts and behaviors. The power of non-verbal communication and body language will be explained in depth in the chapter titled "NLP".

In the chapter "Undetected Mind Control", you will be made aware of how predators with Dark Psychology attempt to exert power and control over your thoughts and behaviors. How a large number of susceptible and vulnerable young people are turning into extremists, at the hands of terrorist groups like ISIS, who are using brainwashing tactics against them. You will also learn how the advent of modern technology has resulted in brainwashing penetrating the world, the likes of which have never been seen before.

You will be able to renew your understanding of the acts of Persuasion and learn some persuasion tactics to help you in your moral endeavors. It might come to you as a shock, that you are being manipulated into making decisions against your self interest. A description and analysis of dark art of Manipulation will open your eyes to the darkness in the world around you. But don't worry, we will end with plenty of tips on how to successfully spot a manipulator and protect yourself from all forms of dark manipulation and from people with active dark psychological traits. A whole lot of self protection tips and techniques with examples, are sprinkled throughout this book for your reference.

There are plenty of books on this subject on the market, thanks again for choosing this one! Every effort was made to ensure it is full of as much useful information as possible, please enjoy!

Chapter 1: The Basics of Dark Psychology

Have you ever been in a situation where you felt somebody is getting the better side of the deal and you cannot seem to fight it? Have you been convinced into doing something which in hindsight seems very unlike yourself? Have you been in a relationship where you knew the person was wrong for you but they always had a majestic hold on you and kept you pulling down in their gravity? If you answered yes to any of these questions, then you have experienced the science and arts of Dark Psychology first hand. Keep on reading because you are going to learn about a whole new dimension of human Psychology that you encounter in your everyday life and need to protect yourself from it!

You do not need to be a science expert to understand the different aspects of Dark Psychology. Now most of us have a general understanding on Psychology as study of general human behavior, how we think, how we act and how we interact; but if the concept of Dark Psychology is new to you, in layman terms, it's some kind of "black magic" that people with powerful influences use to prey upon you to get what they desire, using the tactics of manipulation, coercion and persuasion.

Dark Psychology is the study of innate human behavioral patterns as it relates to the psychological nature of people to victimize other humans and living creatures. Understanding the inherent thoughts, feelings and perceptions of humans that leads to human predatory behavior is at the heart of Dark Psychology studies. All of the humanity is capable of carrying out such criminal and deviant acts and while most of us successfully inhibit and overcome these impulses, a few amongst us embrace these tendencies and commit heinous acts against others. The assumption here is that this predatory behavior is almost always driven by a goal and rationale with a motive but in few of those instances people brutally victimize others with no purposive intent and act on sheer impulse.

Dark Psychology postulates that all of the mankind has a repertoire of malicious intent toward others. It can be a fleeting thought that loses ground before turning into actions or intense psychopathic behavior lacking any rationale what so ever. This is often referred to as the Dark Continuum. The Dark Continuum is a spectrum within which all criminal, sadistic and violent behaviors of the human psyche fall, including thoughts, feelings and actions committed against and/or experienced by individuals. The Dark Continuum can range from severe to mild manifestation and from purpose driven to purposeless. The physical manifestation of Dark Psychology more often than not fall to the right of the Dark Continuum with high severity. On the other hand, the psychological manifestations of Dark Psychology lie to the left of the Dark Continuum, but could potentially be just as destructive as the physical manifestations. Rather than acting as a scale of severity, ranging from bad to worse, Dark Continuum provides a classification of victimization considering the thoughts and actions perpetrated. Farthest to the right of the Dark Continuum is the Dark Singularity.

Singularity can be defined as a point or region where space and time are distorted by the gravitational forces and is assumed to be the center of a black hole which is so dense that even light cannot escape it. Similarly, the Dark Singularity is considered to be the absolute center of the universe of Dark Psychology. It's composed of pure evil and unadulterated malevolence. Only an advance and severe psychopathic individual who viciously victimizes others with purposeless actions comes closest to the Dark Singularity. Human behavior is inherently purpose driven so the Dark Singularity is a theoretical destination not within the grasp of humanity. It can only be approached with no arrival. Alfred Adler was an exemplary psychologist and doctor with contemporaries with the likes of Sigmund Freud and Carl Jung as well as an incredible philosopher. Adler posits that all of the human behavior is purpose driven, from the moment we are born to our death everything we think, feel or do has a purpose to it. Adler believed that even malevolent behavior serves a purpose for the actor and acts of benevolence serve the person in form of acceptance by their loved ones and the community. Healthy functional human behavior is driven by a strong need of people to be accepted by others and have a sense of belonging. Human beings are highly sociable and when people lose their perception of society they tend to move to further away from their inherent purpose of being part of a social construct.

Now nobody is born a criminal but we are all born with a reservoir of malevolence that can be manifested into our being, either due to our horrid circumstances of needing something as basic as food and shelter to the riches of the world or due to terrible and gut wrenching life experiences that stoke our dark side into action. But on some occasions people succumb to their dark sides completely and commit heinous crimes without any goal. Their dark side takes over control and they act criminally not for money, power or retribution. These are the sadistic elements of our society that act upon their predatory behavior of hurting other severely with no mercy. As humans increasingly become discouraged and isolated from the society, their tendency to commit violent and heinous acts against others gets stronger. An instant example would be the narcissistic psychopath who is extremely selfish, seeks pleasure in victimizing others and is motivated to take advantage of others without a hint of remorse for his actions. Adler referred to the trinity of human experience comprising of our thoughts, feelings and behaviors as "constellation" and added subjective processing to this system to establish his second theoretical tenet of Dark Psychology. For example, you use sunglasses to protect your eyes from the harmful rays of the sun and filter the incoming light. Think of your eyes ae true reality and sunglasses represent your filtering mechanism that distorts the reality of harsh sun light, similarly, your perceptual sunglasses tend to alter how you assess and interpret information to make required responses.

"The greater the feeling of inferiority that has been experienced, the more powerful is the urge to conquest and the more violent the emotional agitation." Alfred Adler

Dark Psychology attempts to address the human

consciousness that allows for and may even propel predatory behavior. Few characteristic features of these behavioral tendencies include lack of rationale and motivation, its universality and its lack of predictability. Humans evolved from other animals and today we are the most superior being on the planet but for better or worse we are not completely removed from our animal instincts and thereby our innate predatory nature. The three prime instincts known to mankind are Sex, aggression and instinctual drive to sustain the human race for generations to come. Charles Darwin's theory of "survival of the fittest" is the grandest law of the planet which requires procreation and sustenance of the progenies. So all forms of life engage in their ultimate goal to make more of their own kind and ensure the longevity of their genes. Whether you are the lion king of the jungle trying to win his Pride for the mating rights or an ordinary human being wanting to extend his family name to a new generation; the survival of our progeny requires a marked and protected territory which in turn requires aggression to withstand and win the survival battles. Surely you have seen one or more wildlife documentaries with a helpless innocent deer being ripped to shreds by bigger and stronger predatory animals and surely you were always rooting for the deer to make a fortunate escape but this act of violence is in complete accordance with our evolutionary model. The predator kills for food which is required for self-preservation. Often male animals need to fight and kill one another to come to power and mark their territory but all these violent acts are explained and ordained by the evolutionary model; these acts are not application of Dark Psychology.

Our ability to process complex information and gain perspective has made us the paragon of life forms and also the acme of practicing brutality. With great power comes great responsibility and the only known applications of Dark Psychology on this planet are emanating from the human behavior. Only humans tend to prey on other humans without the reason for procreation and for unaccountable motivations. All of us are aware of the brutalities committed against humans by other humans motivated by the urge to procreate, survive, gain means or territory but most of us have also become increasingly aware of crimes committed for reasons that had no basis and yielded only by the psychopathic tendencies of the predator. Dark Psychology posits that there is something within the human psyche that dictates our actions and is occasionally against the evolutionary model. This phenomenon has been known to mankind every since we evolved with power of thoughts and perception. There is no man that walked this earth in the past, present or future who doesn't have a reservoir of malevolence and doesn't possess a dark side to him. It is just an inexplicable part of who we are and there is no substantial justification for it.

People with prominent Dark Psychology are prone to committing heinous acts like rape and murder with no purpose or cause. It's almost impossible to be able to predict who amongst us will act on their dangerous impulses and even more unpredictable is the extent some will go in acting on these impulses. Dark Psychology attempts to understand and study these dangerous elements that bring people to act as predators and seek out human prey without any cause or purpose. The concept of purpose driven human behavior is vital to the understanding of the Dark Psychology.

We have all fallen victim to Dark Psychology guided predator in some form in our lifetime, so do not feel humiliated. We all possess a dark side which is not well understood and Dark Psychology surrounds us waiting to pounce on us in a moment of weakness. Think about it, humans have enjoyed hunting helpless animals as a sport leading to senseless cruelty against animals. This act of violence against animals is both vicious and psychopathic but normalized by the society. Recent studies have suggested that people with a history of animal abuse have a higher probability of committing violence against human beings. Hunting for recreation brings a euphoria to the predator that if often addictive. Predatory animals kill other animals in search of food or territory, as evident by the food chain and dictated by the evolutionary model of "survival of the fittest". But humans with their reservoir of malicious intent are always at the cusp of losing to these Dark Psychology forces and commit violence against humans.

A milder side of the Dark Continuum can be observed in the increasing levels of violence in children's video games which have now taken over the traditional play time in the fresh air to cozy comfort of their couches. Vandalism of other's property is also a part of Dark Continuum, where humans deliberately damage and destroy another's property willfully and maliciously with no purpose. Children's inclination to play violent video games and deface a property are mild in comparison to overt acts of violence, but are unambiguous examples of the universal human condition of possessing a dark side. Humanity struggles to acknowledge the presence of Dark Psychology even though these dark factors quietly lurk beneath the surface in our human forms.

Some religions even define Dark Psychology as an actual entity that they refer and sometimes revere as Satan. Existence of demons is reasoned to be real culprit leading to malicious and violent actions, in some cultures. Some cultures have defined Dark Psychology as a condition of human psyche or produced by genetic traits inherited from one generation to another. Our inclination to deflect the very idea of dark forces within us arises from the goal of self-preservation within the boundaries of social norms. Thus, often in some religions the underlying intent of violence committed against others is portrayed as commanded by God to accuse the sinners and to carry out God's punishment.

Remember, Dark Psychology is like a spider's web

attempting to capture all previous theories of human victimization and communicate them to others inspiring awareness, and encouraging self-awareness. The more you you can grasp and comprehend Dark Psychology, the better you are prepared to reduce your chances of being a victim at the hands of human predators. Here are the key principles to help you fully grasp Dark Psychology.

1. Dark Psychology is the study of innate human behavioral patterns as it relates to the psychological nature of people to victimize other humans and living creatures. The notion being the closer a person draws to pristine evil, the odds of them having a purpose in motivation diminished by manifolds.

2. All of the mankind has a repertoire of malicious intent toward others. It can be a fleeting thought that loses ground before turning into actions or intense psychopathic behavior lacking any rationale what so ever. People all over the world from different society and culture possess this

facet of human condition. Even the most benevolent people to have inhabited this planet have known this dark side within but never acted upon it.

3. Dark Psychology can easily be overlooked in its latent form due to its high propensity of being misinterpreted as abnormal psychopathy. History is loaded with examples of this latent tendency being activated into destructive behavior. Dark Psychology posits that there is a continuum of severity ranging from mere thoughts of acting violent to severely victimizing others without any purpose or motivation.

4. Dark Psychology suggests that the all humans have potential for violence and various internal and external factors affect the probability of this potential to manifest into dangerous behavior. These behaviors often function with no motivation or rationale and are predatory in nature which makes Dark Psychology a solely human phenomenon.

5. To make the society as safer place for all, understanding of the underlying causes and triggers of Dark Psychology is extremely crucial. Learning the concepts of Dark Psychology will empower people to recognize and reduce the dangers in its influence. Grasping these tenets of Dark Psychology fits our evolutionary model of "survival of the fittest".

Now that you have a basic understanding of what is Dark Psychology and how its prevalent in our world, you are one step closer to being able to protect yourself and people around you from being a victim. Keep reading because we will peel this onion and uncover the Dark Psychology secrets in great detail to arm you against potential predators. You will experience increased self-awareness and be inspired to educate others on how to guard themselves from falling victim at the hands of those few possessed by the Dark Psychology forces.

Chapter 2: Historical Revelation of Dark Psychology

Since the beginning of recorded history, monstrosity inflicted by humans on their own species is abundantly occurring. Although atrocious, it never fails to astonish how apparently decent individuals could possibly allow or even participate in such horrendous acts. Historical evidences of such horrifying acts against humanity are infinitely occurring. Prominent example of such act that left a lasting impact on the world today is the holocaust during World War II that killed hundreds of thousands of innocent Jews as victims of systematic genocide. Nazis described Jews as *Untermenshen*, or subhumans, and were excluded from the system of moral rights and obligations that fabricate the society. More than seventy million people were reported dead in the World War II, most of them were civilians and millions died in combat. So many were burned alive by incendiary bombs and then the nuclear weapons scarred the planet. It's the manifestation of Dark Psychology within people in powerful positions that made this carnage possible. Hitler's rise to power in Nazi Germany could be attributed in part to his ability to normalize the Dark Psychology within the community by dehumanizing his enemies. It enabled one group of people to treat another with zero perception of their humanity. It's definitely wrong to kill humans, but easily permissible to exterminate a rodent. During the Holocaust and over the course of the Third Reich, Hitler ordered a series of experiments to be conducted on Jews, Russian, Roma and other persecuted groups. These experiments were conducted in concentration camps and mostly resulted in disfigurement or permanent disability and often into death. Hitler's euthanasia program allowed over 200,000 mentally or physically disabled people, deemed unfit to live were gassed to death.

Particularly disturbing experiments included attempts to genetically manipulate twins; sterilization; premeditative exposure to harmful gasses; nerve, muscle and bone transplantation among other horrendous crimes against humanity. After the end of World War II and defeat of Germany, these crimes were tried as part of the Nuremberg trial held in 1946, twenty doctors were accused of crimes against humanity and ultimately the Nuremberg Code of medical ethics was established. The trail provided gruesome details of the experiments conducted on innocent people, who were treated worse than animals and merely served as human guinea pigs for their murderers. Some were deprived of oxygen to stimulate high altitude parachute jumps. Some were exposed to mustard gas causing severe external and internal burns to the victims. Some were frozen to death and other exposed to bites from malaria-infected mosquitos. Some had their flesh incised to simulate wounds. Some had shards to glass and wood shavings inserted into them and then their blood vessels were tied off. Some were introduced to bacteria that in turn induced gangrene. People were coerced into drinking seawater, infected with typhus and other life-threatening diseases. Some were even poisoned and burned with phosphorus. These acts were immensely graphic and sure to enrage most readers. The Dark Psychology that went behind the perpetrators of these acts is unspeakably terrifying. To the Nazis, all Jews were rats that could be easily and inhumanely preyed upon and were often represented as parasitic organisms.

In 1943 Hitler proclaimed, *"Today international Jewry is the ferment of decomposition of peoples and states, just as it was in antiquity. It will remain that way as long as peoples do not find the strength to get rid of the virus."*

Dehumanizing the enemy allowed German soldier and officers to act in accordance with the Nazi's vision of warfare of no mercy. In ancient Chines and Egyptian literature enemies are often referred as subhuman creatures. Unfortunately, dehumanization during World War II was not restricted to the lethal program of racial hygiene implemented by the Nazis in Germany.

The dehumanizing rhetoric of the Stalin's Red Army described Germans as "ersatz men", meaning "two-legged animals who have mastered the technique of war". The Russian-Jewish poet Ilya Ehrenburg made significant contribution to hype up this propaganda writing "If you kill one German, kill another — there is nothing more amusing for us than a heap of German corpses." With the defeat of Germany in World War II, the Red Army wreaked havoc into the Germany from the east. In just a night 72 women were killed and most women had been raped. A witness who had survived and made it to the west reported of a village girl who had been raped by an entire tank squadron for more than 12 hours. Some of the victims had been crucified and man was brutally shot and then fed to the pigs.

A more recent example of the manifestation of Dark Psychology in our society is the Rwandan Genocide of 1994, in which over 800,000 people were murdered by Hutu extremists within a short time span of 100 days. Majority of Rwandans are Hutus but the Tutsi minority had predominantly controlled the country. Hutus targeted their political opponents, irrespective of their ethnic origin and not just the members of the Tutsi community. Militias were provided with list of government opponents to be slaughtered along with their families. Some men even killed their own Tutsi wives with the fear of their own death. Most Rwandans owned machetes that they used to kill Tutsis at the roadblocks set up by militia. People were required to have their ethnic group listed on their ID cards to aid in this massacre. Thousands of Tutsi women who survived the slaughter were taken away and used as sex slaves. Hutus fed into the dehumanizing rhetoric of stripping people of their basic human traits. Tutsis were referred to as cockroaches and Hutu extremists circulated propaganda egging people to "weed out the cockroaches", often declaring the death of prominent figures on radio. The conflicts between Hutus and Tutsis crossed boundaries of multiple African countries with estimation of five million deaths until 2003 and to this day some armed groups are still active near Rwanda's border.

The Holocaust and the Rwandan Genocide provided a gut wrenching insight into the world of Dark Psychology with one or more individuals with enthusiasm for sadism and inclination on its usage, wrote some of the horrendous events of human history. These events occurred on such massive scale that the world was a witness to its everyday progress with daily newspaper headlines. Another event to have dominated newspaper headlines was the case of infamous and notorious serial killer Ted Bundy. The story of Ted Bundy and his brutalities is that of a textbook psychopathic killer on every account. The amount of media coverage given to him and his crimes is almost fascinating and largely owed to Bundy's willingness to appear for interviews and offer insights into his actions. Bundy was linked to close to 100 murders but was only charged with 30 and there is still no confirmation on the total number of murders he committed. Bundy spent significant time on death row after being sentenced to death. Detailed psychological analysis of Ted Bundy was carried out to understand the possible motivation behind the vicious acts of the most dangerous serial killer to have ever been incarcerated.

A striking aspect of Ted Bundy's lengthy murder career happens to be how it evolved over course of time. Bundy admitted that his initial crimes were opportunistic with sloppy execution but he evolved his methods over time and become more organized, elaborate and careful with his approach. Bundy was often described as "shape shifter" owing to his ability to alter his physical appearance with subtle yet comprehensive misdirection. He was just as skillful at hiding his true motivation and methods, deceiving his victims not just physically but also psychologically. Deception is one of the many traits of Dark Psychology. Extensive study of Bundy's deceptive ways provided valuable insight into the dark psychological traits of serial killers. It's well established that most people and his victims found him to be attractive and charming. Bundy had a very clear understanding of power of perception and that of public image. So he mastered a façade of charm and desirability with no inner truth to the matter. Think about it, the man was able to invoke comfort and attraction in his victim moments before assaulting and killing them in cold blood, portraying the emotional coldness of men like Bundy carrying out some of the most sadistic crimes known to the mankind. Psychopaths like Bundy inherently tend to detach themselves from their reality and thereby the consequences of their actions. Bundy displayed highly intense sadism and narcissism in the way he tortured his victims, took pictures of their dead bodies and often referred to himself in third person.

"The term 'serial killings' means a series of three or more killings, not less than one of which was committed within the United States, having common characteristics such as to suggest the reasonable possibility that the crimes were committed by the same actor or actors." United States Federal Bureau of Investigation

Another such Narcissist to have made his mark on the history was self proclaimed Russian faith healer, Grigori Rasputin. The infamous "mad monk" perverted the Khlysty (Flagellants) beliefs, stating that prolonged debauchery that let to sexual exhaustion was the best way to feel near to God. His lascivious reputation earned him the last name

Rasputin, believed to be Russian for "licentious". After failing to become a monk and marrying Proskovya Fyodorovna Dubrovina at the age of 19, he abandoned his home and family and wandered to Mount Athose and Jerusalem while sustaining himself off the peasant's donation, proclaiming to possess mystic abilities of predicting the future and healing the sick. Rasputin eventually arrived in St. Petersburg, where at the time the court circles were delving into mysticism for entertainment and therefore, welcomed Rasputin with open arms. The Russian royal family, Nicholas and Alexandra, summoned Rasputin for his mystic healing powers during one of their son's bleeding episodes. Rasputin succeeded in easing boy's discomfort and warned the royalties that their destiny was irrevocably tied to his own, thereby making himself as a staunch ally of the imperial family and highly influenced the state affairs. Outside the royal court, Rasputin kept up with his salacious habits, preaching that his physical contact had profound purifying and healing effect. Rasputin's inexplicable ability to be both a devil and angel in the same moment, only scratched the surface of the devastating influence of his personality. He succeeded in inducing a trancelike state of suggestibility in his victims and happens to be the first anecdotal usage of hypnosis ever recorded. It was believed that Rasputin could easily induce deep feelings of calm and relaxation in his victims and to date serve as the harbinger of modern faith healers. Rasputin had mastered the art of covert emotional intelligence, explained subsequently in this book in details, where his victims were oblivious to the control and power he held on them. It simply came across as if he had a mystic aura that people just succumbed to. The Dark Psychology of charismatic influence is widely observed in the modern world today. These predators attract mass following by creating a perception that they possess some secret knowledge that could pave way to the higher self by simply feigning spirituality.

The Milgram Obedience Study of 1960, revealed

that ordinary people upon encouragement from an authoritative figure, were willing to torture other humans and in this experiment they used potentially lethal levels of electricity. The subjects were reported to be far more obedient than anticipated. Milgram advised his subjects that they were part of an important experiment that could advance the cause of science in order to impart a perception of social value to his study. This experiment once again served as a reminder that there is a reservoir of malevolence within all of us and given the opportunity these dark factors can take over our personality. However, the results of the Milgram experiment were underscored by that of the Stanford Prison Experiment of the 1971.

One of the extremely controversial studies in the history of social psychology and by extension Dark Psychology was the Stanford Prison Experiment. Middle class college student served as willing participants and were selected based on their family backgrounds as well as their physical and mental health histories. The participants were then grouped into prisoners and guards, simply through a coin toss. The guards were not provided any directions on their operation and instinctively started humiliating and psychologically abusing the prisoners within 24 hours of the start of the experiment. The prisoners, in turn, took the abuse with little to no protest and acted docile. The human behavior displayed by both the groups was so extreme that the experiment was terminated just after six days, instead of the slated two-week period. The Standard Experiment succeeded in revealing the ease with which ordinary people when given powerful authority could transform into ruthless oppressors within hours. The Stanford Experiment is often used as evidence of primitive dark impulses that lurk within all of us and can turn a completely normal human being into a tyrant, with a little nudge.

It is easy to deduce from these experiments, that humans can easily be swayed into dehumanizing others, which serves as a loophole in human psyche to justify their predatory behavior. Murder and torture are universal taboo but killing "animals" for food or even sport is acceptable in most cultures. Neuroscience research conducted by Princeton university showed that dehumanizing others turned off the regions of our brains corresponding to empathy and turned on regions associated with disgust. When people move towards the extreme ends of the Dark Continuum and lose sense of self, not fearing death, they are more prone to committing crimes against humanity. The latest example of these inclinations can be observed in use of violence against Muslims and Mexican immigrant in the United States of America or the use of radical rationalization by terrorist groups like ISIS.

Terrorist organizations often use brainwashing to recruit and retain followers who are fed the extreme religious or political rhetoric. The ease of availability and usage of modern technology has fueled the extremist agenda of these organizations.

Historically brainwashing often required physical proximity, gatherings in cult headquarters or a secure location. But with the advent of Internet, terror organizations can remotely reach a massive audience simply with few clicks of a button. Frequently referred to as viral videos, propaganda videos are released by these terror mongers as the modern tool of brainwashing. The likes of the brainwashing features released unleashed on this generation are uncanny on multiple levels, these organizations still follow their tried and tested methods of indoctrination that have existed for centuries. The technologically spiked innovative methodologies of brainwashing has followers willingly and blindly committing to act violently at the risk of their own lives. Suicide bombings are being increasingly reported at common social places like cafes, night clubs or supermarkets. It would be foolish to underestimate the severity of this problem that's threatened our society. The biggest loss facing our society is that of our young generation living their life on Internet and are highly susceptible to these brain washing techniques. Young men and even women leave their families and home behind, forsaking a comfortable life and familiar world only to die in a foreign war. The extremist propaganda has instigated the mentally deranged individuals into carrying out crimes against their own communities and nation, resulting in "lone wolf" attacks.

With the great power of Internet, our responsibility to ensure its ethical use has increased manifolds. The terror organization have managed to update their application of classic brainwashing principles to function over the realms of Internet. Vulnerable individuals can be easily found by those predators who wish to poison these individuals with their extremist views. Anyone can seamlessly track down a target who is susceptible to the incendiary views held by the terrorist organization against a community or nation. These targeted individuals are then assigned to specific members of the group in order to effectively influence them to agree and believe in their propaganda. These recruiters then apply the basic and age old principles of brainwashing on their prey slowly and methodically. This process often takes significant time to sink into the target's psyche. The terror group often conceals objectionable thoughts and acts, until the victim is primed to be open minded to the polarizing rhetoric of the organization.

The modern terror organizations often employ the tried and tested methodologies of presenting their rhetoric as a utopian solution to personal woes of the victim. The terror organizations promoting radical Islamist view or right-wing racism are often using the same tactic to lure and retain their followers. Their message to the victims vilifies the society and proposes their own narrative as the antidote to all that is wrong with the world today. Misleading videos and images are frequently used to bolster their own portrayal of injustice in the society, manufacturing a heavily biased version of life. As a result, the victim often feels fortunate and grateful to have been welcomed and accepted by the terrorist organization. They are fragmented from the society at an early age with a highly impressionable mindset and then brainwashed to commit vicious crimes against humanity. The terror organization use the grievances of youth going through identity crisis to their own advantage. They trigger the dark factors of vulnerable youth to unleash the monster within and cross to the extremes of the Dark Continuum. The Dark Psychology of these terrorist groups to breed hatred within their community, criminalizing the youth and using them as their weapon of mass destruction. The antidote to save our youth lies in the palms of our leaders and figures of authority, who should aim to uphold the values of inclusiveness, respect and pluralism. They must abandon inflammatory speeches and warlike narratives that feed the hate speech of the extremist groups. The fight against segregation must be translated into inclusive policy addressing the vulnerable community and the Muslim community,

who are also victims of this radical rhetoric echoing
the world today.

Chapter 3: Dark Psychology and Human Behavior

The social sciences, including Psychology, Sociology, Anthropology and Economics are studying the human behavior to establish our ancient history and define the course of our future generations. A deeper understanding of how humans act, plan, memorize and make decisions is of paramount significance to the study of Dark Psychology. Change is the most constant law of the nature and with the being said, the human behavior and mentality has certainly evolved over time in conjunction with our physical appearance. With that being said, every individual defines themselves through their own life experiences and the environment they grow up in. There is a baseline of common human behavioral patterns that resemble the fundamental characteristics of all human beings. Our environment is the single most influencing criteria that dictates how we develop over time, not only physically but also mentally. Our environment primarily comprises of other human beings that we interact with on a regular basis, our lifestyle, our neighborhood, the country and the social values inspired by the leader of the country among other external factors. For example, our parents provide us the with the first human interaction right after we are born. Their habits and behaviors directly feed into our mental and physical growth. Individuals with strong ties to their family growing up are more likely to contribute to the success of the overall community, owing to their strong sense of camaraderie. Therefore, its often observed that individuals with disturbing childhood and/or coming from a broken home are more vulnerable in acting violent or committing crimes against their own communities.

According to the study of Dark Psychology, the reservoir of malevolence exists within all our psyches and can be triggered into taking violent actions against other humans. Our social environment tends to be the most powerful trigger and can just as easily generate negative behavior and actions as positive behavior and actions. Individuals of low means who have spent their childhood struggling to meet their basic needs of food and shelter, often grow up with a distaste for the society they live in. They believe their society and community failed to provide them with equal opportunities furthering their miseries. The economic disparity that exists in the world today is getting worse by the day. The rich are getting richer and poor are getting poorer, struggling to get access to the basic human needs. People are trapped in poverty with little to no chance of climbing up the economic scale. The unequal distribution of opportunities in turn leads to unequal income of different groups of the society. In the United States, the income gap between the rich and poor has grown remarkably, by every major statistical measure, for more than past 30 years. The current income disparity in America is astonishing, the top 10% averages more than 9 times the income of the bottom 90% while the top 1% has an average income of over 39 times more than the income of the bottom 90%. If that is not disturbing enough, the fact is the nation's top 0.1% percent report average income more than 188 times as the bottom 90%. This pronounced disproportion of income and by extension opportunities eats up the morale of the poor working class individuals, who are working two jobs to pay their rent and bring food to the table. These perpetually oppressed minorities are associated with poor public health and increased crime rate.

Our physical and mental health are directly related. A healthy body bears a healthy mind and vice versa.

In the face of increasing food prices and lower income, economically unequal societies experience suppressed growth. The highly disadvantaged members of the society are more likely to suffer from resentment and hostility, as a direct result of their economic handicap or fierce competition over skimpy jobs or resources. This resentment often translates into higher propensity for criminal behavior. Our thought process works bilaterally, we are always weighing in immediate and log term pros and cons of our actions. Inequality often leads to bigger incentives to commit crimes, in comparison to obtaining resources lawfully, even when you account for the risk of punishments. Limited methods are available to the disadvantaged members of the unequal society and illegal methods of getting access to resources may provide better return in the long run. The pronounced disparity between rich and poor tends to increase crime by massive reduction in the law enforcement spending in low-income areas. Poor neighborhoods and countries lack sufficient funding for the police than their rich counterparts, resulting in less effective law enforcement or higher number of low income police officers susceptible to bribes.

A highly disproportionate occurrence rates of certain kinds of illnesses are endured but the impoverished members of the society. Limited access to healthy food and quality health care result in less effective and lower income work force, higher illnesses, higher mortality rates and higher health health care costs, perpetually deepening poverty for the oppressed societies. During the early 1990s, the term "food desert" originated in Scotland, in the context of a public sector housing report. Food deserts can singularly characterize economically unequal society, afflicted by the scarcity of healthy and affordable food. Several of the developed Western countries including Canada, Australia, New Zealand and the United Kingdom have reported occurrences of food deserts. In America, the limited access to fresh foods is associated with rampant obesity and high rate of diet-related diseases among the impoverished members of the society. The American people living below the federal poverty line are two times more likely to die from diet related diseases like Diabetes. In turn, the poor are disproportionately burdened with higher health care costs to be tackled with a less effective workforce, reinforcing the wealth disparity.

Dark Psychology posits that the predatory instinct within all of us is more often than not driven by a purpose or motive. An elite group of scientists from the Northeastern University recently reported that 93% of human behavior is predictable. The experiment conducted, by the physicist Albert-László Barabási and his team, studied the mobility patterns of anonymous cell-phone users. The conclusion was that the human mobility surprisingly follows regular patterns, in complete contrast with the general perception that all human actions are random and unpredictable. Barabási and his team, proposed that the future whereabouts of an individual in the next hour could be predicted based on their previous trajectory. They also discovered that the length of the distance travelled by the individual had no impact on the predictability of their future travel. So the team reported 93% predictability with people that tend to stay close to home as well as people that tend to regularly travel long distances. The predictability and regularity of individual moment transcended through the wide variety of demographics. It turns out the heterogeneity of our age, gender, native language, and even population density did not alter the predictability of human behavior. Human mobility directly impacts the urban planning and traffic engineering of the country. This research could help drive the public health and urban development by scientifically predicting people's movement in near future.

Our scientifically advanced society has tapped into the world of wearable technology to explore the unknown and deep seated secrets of the human brain and mind. The researchers now have access to multi modal data acquisition and analysis to fuel the speed and accuracy of their studies. Our brain has a highly complex set of neural network and patterns that support our natural, active and ever evolving behavior and cognition. The systematic observation and interpretation of the functioning of the brain poses a difficult challenge. Human brain structures have evolved to support the complex cognitive processes that are targeted at optimizing the outcomes of all our actions.

The three major components of human behavior are actions, cognition and emotions. An action is real life manifestation that can be observed with our eyes and measured by psychological sensors. Our actions lead to transition from one state to another. Cognition pertains to our mental capability of though processing, both verbally and non verbally. Emotions are characterized by intense mental activity that cannot be observed directly, resulting in a feeling based on reasoning or knowledge and yielding to a conscious experience. These three cogs of our psyche, namely action, cognition and emotions, running as a well oiled machine, enable us to perceive the world around us and make appropriate responses to our surroundings. It is challenging to determine the cause and effect of this relay. An action can result in a specific emotion accompanied by an internal realization (cognition), which in turn can trigger a different emption and bring us into a whole new action. Our observable actions are certainly driven by our emotions and cognition. Humans actively move their body to manifest cognitive goals and desires or to achieve a specific mental state.

Our cognition is always evolving and our existing mindset adapts, merges and integrates the new information we experience over the course of our lives, to predict how changes in the current environment may be influenced by your actions. Our cognition helps steer our actions in a timely manner which are appropriate to our environmental conditions. Human mind can dynamically respond to a stimuli based on our intentions and available instructions. Humans can respond to the same stimulus in a variety of ways, in order to be able to respond to similar stimuli consistently, our minds maintain long lasting stimulus-response relationship. For example, once your mind has perceived a person as a friend or a foe, it taps back into its existing stimulus-response relationship to determine if you need to react to the person in a friendly manner or not. Cognitions that lack any physical interaction with the surrounding and are completely abstract in nature can still be experienced by the body. Take a moment and imagine that you are out for a run in your neighborhood, the stimuli that you just experienced triggers the same brain areas that are associated with the limb movement as when you are actually out on a run. You must have heard how people practice for an interview while looking in a mirror or repeat positive affirmations to help with their confidence. These actions help us rehearse our working memory by triggering the same brain areas that are involved in speech perception and production, establishing a consistent stimulus-response relationship for future interactions.

Our instincts, reflexes and random movements constitute the fundamental units of our behavior. Random movements can be regarded as the primary ingredients for largely integrated human behavioral patterns. Human movements and impulses that do not appear to be directed at a defined adjustment end are considered random. Our predetermined neural connections and physical structure, dictate and restrain the extent of our random movement like turning our heads, moving our arms and fingers and even vocal acts like crying or shrieking. These types of behavior are not adaptive in a true sense as they are limited by the structural characteristic of the person and cannot be entirely deemed as random. Since random behavior is not purposive, it is a characteristic of early childhood and any such behavior observed in older children or adults is often linked to temporary nervousness or chronic neural disorganization. In individuals on the extremes of the Dark Continuum, this random behavior leads to violent inclinations and psychopathic tendencies.

Human beings and all animals with nervous system possess the simple behavioral unit called the reflex. The uniquely defining characteristic of the reflex is that it results in a definite and predictable response, that is common to all of the human species. For example, when being pricked by a pin our immediate response is withdrawal and that response is standard across the men and women, child and adult, or rich and poor. The reflex is in no sense purposive and supremely unconscious behavioral process. In a standardized environmental situation, the reflex results into consistent response, imparting stability to the behavior of the organism. People that are unable to respond consistently to the same stimulus suffer from disintegration. Our reflexes provide us economical and unconscious mechanisms to address our simpler and routine day to day affairs, primarily the physiological ones. Now you must be wondering how reflexes and random behavior are related. The differences between the two categories are difficult to understand, but in general, reflexes are more specific and adaptive than random behavior. However, random behavior is often influenced by our reflexes.

Unlike reflexes our instincts are adaptive and not purposive. Human instincts tend to be much more complex than the reflexes, although, similar to the reflexes, instincts are inherited and definite resulting in specific and defined response to a particular stimulus. Our instincts operate independent from our consciousness and any correlation of the two can only appear, if the original behavioral pattern has been modified or is being interfered by the given situation. The complex social world of the human beings with rapidly changing environment increases the possibility of modifications to the rigid basis of our instincts.

Human instincts are offer characterized as a combination of reflexes which are predetermined by biological selection regardless of the environment and serve a direct function in the adjustment process. Majority of the complex animal instincts do not survive in the human beings and only the instincts that serve physiological functions associated with eating, breathing and reproduction are relatively intact. Thanks to our instincts when sensing immediate danger, we jump into action and run away from the situation. The Dark Psychological traits of an individual can diminish these self preserving instincts, allowing them to commit heinous crimes being fully aware of the risk of the punishment. They are consciously aware that their actions are negative and wrong but their dark side encourages them to continue their endeavor.

Human behavior is acquired by learning, our decision to take action or withhold a certain behavior is dependent on the benefits and risks associated with our activity. The "Prospect Theory", published in 1979, by Daniel Kahneman and Amos Tversky, is touted as the most influential psychological theories on decision making. Prospect theory is a behavioral model that demonstrated are loss-averse and process expected utility relative to their current state instead of the absolute outcomes. Humans are willing to take on additional risk in order to avoid a loss, since we dislike losses more than equivalent gains. Prospect theory was developed by framing risky choices and concluded that individuals make decisions based on perceived gains rather than perceived losses. When given choices offer the same outcome but are presented differently, an individual will most certainly choose the option that offers perceived gains. For example, the joy you experience if someone gave you $50 upfront should be equal to a situation where you gained $100 but somehow lost $50, as both situations lead to a net gain of $50. But most people view the single gain of $50 than the gain and loss scenario. Prospect theory proposed that loss causes a much greater emotional impact on an individual than the equivalent amount of gain. In 1995, another study was conducted on Olympic medal winners which demonstrated that the bronze medal winners seemed on average far happier than the silver medal winners. The silver medalists tend to focus on almost winning gold and any alternate outcome, including the silver medal is perceived as a loss. On the other hand, the bronze medalists focus on not winning a medal at all and therefore, any outcome above not winning is perceived as a gain. Prospect theory, also called as "loss-aversion" theory revealed that human process information in an illogical way by valuing gains and losses differently. The Prospect theory also laid the foundations for Daniel Kahneman's other theories, as published in his book titled "Thinking, Fast and Slow". Kahneman proposed that humans possess two decision making systems. The first system is fast but relatively inaccurate and the second system is slow but much more accurate. Decisions like buying food products, to making career choices are carried out by either of these two systems.

The famous Austrian neurologist, Sigmund Freud (1856-1939), was the founder of psychoanalysis. Freud's theory of psychoanalysis can explain human behavior and is used as a method to treat mental illness. Psychoanalysis is often considered a theory of the human psyche, a visual for social and cultural interpretation and a therapy to relieve mental illness. In 1873, Freud attended the University of Vienna to study medicine and worked at the Vienna General Hospital post graduation. He collaborated with physician Josef Breuer, who had been studying hysterical symptoms of a patient named Bertha Pappenheim- or "Anna O.". Breuer allowed Anna to lapse into a state resembling autohypnosis wherein she talked about the initial manifestations of her symptoms. The very act of verbalization, "the talking cure" or "chimney sweep", was found to be extremely cathartic for Anne, who was able to discharge her pent-up emotions, at the root of pathological behavior.

1n 1885, Freud married Martha Bernays, with whom

he had six children, and became a student of the neurologist Jean Charcot in Paris. Charcot's work on hysteria introduced Freud to the possibility that psychological disorders have an origin in the mind rather than the brain. Freud was not able to fully comprehend the implications of Breuer's experiment, for another 10 years, and was still indebted to Charcot's hypnotic methods. A decade later, Freud developed the technique of free association, by encouraging patient to express aloud thoughts and feelings without suppression or self censorship of any kind, to expose unarticulated material from the realm of the psyche called the unconscious. Freud observed that the patient's resistance or defense against the expression of conscious thoughts or conflicts, completely hidden unconscious thoughts that were unavailable to the conscious, posed a challenge in free association of sudden silences, stuttering or other hysterical symptoms. Based on his clinical experience, Freud concluded most of female hysterical symptoms and resisted thoughts had sexual aspect to it. He proceeded to connect the etiology of neurotic symptoms to the same struggle between sexual urges and psychic defenses against it, often leading to an unwitting compromise between the wish and the defense.

In his attempts to establish psychoanalysis as a universal theory, Freud would have to examine male psyche as well, in a condition of normality, so he proceeded to generalize psychoanalysis from his own experience. Freud's self exploration was in fact triggered by the death of his father, Jakob Freud. He felt his long repressed emotions concerning his own family experiences and feelings were being released. In 1897, Freud used the technique of deciphering dreams to reveal the meaning of his emotional discharge. According to Freud, dreams were "the royal road to a knowledge of the unconscious," and his analysis provided a deep understanding of how dreams originate and function. In 1899, he presented his findings in the ground breaking book called "Die Traumdeutung" or "The Interpretation of Dreams". Freud posits that dreams play a pivotal role in the human psychic economy. He called libido as the minds energy, associating it with the volatile human sexual drive, capable of excessive and disturbing power. He stated that the libido functions to gain pleasure and prevent pain, seeking any and all possible outlets and lack of this physical gratification allowed libidinal energy to seek its release through mental channels. Freud claimed that all dreams, were manifestation of these wishes being fulfilled inside the human unconscious as disguised expression. Dreams are the effects of psychological compromises between desires and the conflicts preventing realization of these desires. The Dark Psychology of repressed emotions generating from a trauma or disturbing life events can, therefore, easily manifest into predatory behavior with no apparent rational motivation.

Unlike dreams, seemingly insignificant errors like forgetting names, misreading or slip of tongue (colloquially called Freudian slips) could arise from immediate hostile or egoistic causes and have symptomatic and interpretable importance. The dark factors hiding within our psyche often lead to violent dreams or nightmares and can even manifest in the form of Freudian slips on the dark web of Internet. In the early 1900s, Freud developed a topographical model of the mind and described it using the analogy of an iceberg. He claimed that the mind had three layers, namely, the conscious, preconscious and unconscious. The consciousness was the tip or the surface of the iceberg represented thoughts that are our immediate focus of attention. The layer of the ice just under the water and could made aware of if desired, represented the preconscious, which consists of all the thoughts that can be retrieved from the memory. The last and most critical layer is that of the unconscious, which was deep seated and could not be made aware of.

It is the unconscious that holds the reservoir of malevolence within all of us and primarily causes most of human behavior. The unconscious mind is like a "cauldron" of primitive impulses and potential for violence, which can spring into action as driven by the internal and external factors and manifest into volatile behaviors. The ultimate goal of psychoanalysis is to make the unconscious thoughts and feelings conscious and providing humans the psychological support needed to prevent manifestation of the dark factors within. In 1923, Freud categorized structures of the mind into ID, Ego and Superego. The ID was considered to be the most primitive urges or instincts linked with instant gratification of sexual needs and urges. The superego pertains to social and cultural rules and norms and similar to what we call as "moral compass". The ego refers to the rational and pragmatic of the mind, that strives for self preservation by delaying gratification to suffice the norms of the society and resolve the conflicts between the primitive desires of the ID and the superego.

Freud believed that human behavior and personality

are rooted in the results of the constant conflicts between the ID, ego and superego over the course of our childhood. Individuals with prominent Dark Psychology often struggle with a weak ego which causes imbalances in their mental state and can lead to neurosis and unhealthy behaviors. When our ID or superego overpower ego, we often find ourselves feeling anxious or guilty of our actions and threatened over our well being. Our mind relies on our ego to develop defense mechanisms to deal with our internal struggles and resolved such conflicts with compromise solutions. Ego-defense mechanisms are completely natural and operate unconsciously to strengthen the good feelings and ward off any unpleasant ones. But when these defense mechanisms get out of proportion, they lead to mental instability which can manifest as obsessions, hysteria, anxiety and phobias.

There is a whole repertoire of these defense mechanisms, including denial, projection, sublimation, repression, regression, rationalization, reaction formation, identification with the aggressor and displacement. The most fundamental of all is considered to be repression, when the ego attempts to ward off disturbing and threatening thoughts and ideas from becoming conscious by pushing it down the unconscious part of the mind. These thoughts are suppressed to avoid the feelings of guilt from the superego but in the long term could create anxiety. "Freudian slips" are often manifestation of these repressed memories in the form of dreams or slips of the tongue. For example, victims with hysterical amnesia, where they had either witnessed of performed violet acts can completely forget the acts itself and it occurrence. These individuals have walked over to the extremes of the Dark Continuum and lose any contact with their reality.

Another common defense mechanism is "projection", in which unwanted thoughts, feelings and motives are attributed onto another person and are construed as a threat from the external world. It can be easily observed when an individual, threatened by their own hostile thoughts and feelings believe that these feelings are in fact harbored by the other person. Our superego tells us that hate is a negative feeling and unacceptable so you convince yourself that the hatred inside you for a person, is actually a response to the hatred you experienced from that person. A similar defense mechanism is called "rationalization', where in the ego substitutes a safe and reasonable explanation to make an impulse or an event less threatening. It involves cognitive distortion of the facts in an attempt to self preservation. For example, the terrorist organizations often purport their extremist propaganda as a means to protect their religious, social or political views as a justification for their Dark Psychological behavior and heinous acts.

It is often observed that when the going gets too difficult, our mind responds by refusing to perceive the very existence of those dire circumstances. This is done by invoking the "denial" defense mechanism by the ego, wherein the mind blocks out external events from awareness and fail to acknowledge and accept the reality of the situation. The "denial" defense mechanism is a primitive and potentially dangerous cause aversion from reality can only last so long and disregarding reality can easily allow our mind to underestimate or even ignore the terrible consequences of our unhealthy behavior. The presence of the "denial" mechanism could be as simple as a student failing to admit their lack of required preparedness for an exam or as complex as a wife refusing to acknowledge and confront the obvious signs of her husband's infidelity. More often than not the denial mechanism operates in collaboration with other subtler defense mechanisms. When someone goes beyond denial and behaves completely opposite to how how they think or feel, the "reaction formation" defense mechanism kicks in.

Reaction formation is the adoption of conscious behaviors to overcompensate for a feared socially unacceptable unconscious impulse. It's usually marked by exaggerated behavior like compulsiveness and showiness to curb the anxiety generated by the threatening unconscious thoughts or emotions. The reaction formation mechanism conceals the true motives of the human psyche from the ego while keeping the ID satisfied. For example, a woman bearing an unwanted child, may attempt to curb her guilt for not wanting the child by becoming extremely overprotective and solicitous to convince herself of being a good mother. Freud claimed that men with prejudices against homosexuality, displayed harsh homo-sexual attitude to convince themselves of their heterosexuality and in part to defend against their own homosexual feelings.

Human predators often employ "displacement" to redirect their dark impulses onto a powerless substitute target or prey. Their prey serves as a symbolic substitute of their target and can be a person or an object. In situations where the superego doesn't permit the ID from achieving or fulfilling its desires, the ego settles with an alternative way to expend the psychic energy of the ID. This leads to transfer of energy from a repressed object to a more socially acceptable object but in individuals with prominent and active dark side, the fulfillment of their dangerous desires overpowers the social acceptance of their violent actions. For example, individuals with taboo sexual desires may not be comfortable in their expression with a real persona and may substitute in the form of a fetish.

Most newly married women want to retreat to the security of their parent's home after their first quarrel with their husband. This feeling is prompted by the "regression" defense mechanism, where individuals psychologically go back in time to a period or place when they felt safer. The ego reverts to an earlier stage of development when faces with a stressful situation. Regression is marked by movement back in psychological time to more primitive and abandoned forms of gratification, prompted by the dangers of their current conflicts.

For example, a child undergoing medical treatment in a hospital, may feel the urge to suck on their thumb again or to wet the bed or teenage girls experiencing new social situation with boys might start giggling uncontrollably.

In 1936, psychoanalyst Anna Freud, daughter of Sigmund Freud, published a book titled "The Ego and the Mechanisms of Defense", drawing a distinction between defenses directed to protect the ego from the instinctual demands of the ID and defenses against the affects of these drives. She first described "identification with the aggressor" as a defense mechanism against the painful effects of the external threat, such as disapproval or criticism of an authoritative figure, wherein the victim starts identifying with the source of threat by either adopting the behavior of the predator or by appropriating their aggression. By internalizing the attributes of the threatening figure, victim hopes to instill an emotional connection with the aggressor leading to feelings of empathy to avoid the abuse altogether. The attitude of the victim towards the predator can even translate into feelings of admiration and gratitude. For example, some of the prisoners in the Nazi concentration camps internalized the behavior of guards and abused their own fellow prisoners. An extreme example of identification with the aggressor is Stockholm syndrome or "traumatic bond", wherein the hostages develop favorable feelings and behaviors towards their kidnapper and establish an emotional bond.

The feelings of terror and anxiety of the victims instigates a childlike regression in them, which is experienced as gratitude for the aggressor, whom they start thinking of as provider and tending to their basic needs. The victims feel gratitude towards their captor just for allowing them to be alive, forgetting that their aggressor is the real cause of their suffering. They unconsciously develop an emotional bond with their abuser as a survival strategy, while struggling to understand their situation, creating an empty space within their psyche, which gradually fills up with the characteristics of their aggressor. This trauma in turn triggers a vicious cycle of violence, wherein the victims who don't seek help or are unable to overcome the trauma, are more likely to reproduce the trauma in other people. A classic example would be that of Patty Hearst, who was kidnapped, raped and abused by a left-wing American terrorist group called the Symbionese Liberation Army. In 1976, she was found guilty of joining the same terrorist group of her own volition and sentenced to 35 years in prison on felony charges of committing bank robbery. In 2001 she was pardoned by the President Bill Clinton, on his last day in the office.

Chapter 4: The "Dark Triad"

In 2002, psychologists Paulhus and Williams, coined the term Dark Triad in reference to three offensive yet non-pathological personality variables: Narcissism, Psychopathy and Machiavellianism. The concept of the Dark Triad is relatively new to psychology and paramount to the understanding of Dark Psychology. These three personalities have striking similarities and entail dark, socially destructive characteristics. Prominently negative behavioral tendencies like manipulation, emotional coldness and grandiosity are intricate part of these 3 dark personalities.

The most widely used taxonomy for personality traits is called the "Big Five", which is based on common language descriptors, suggesting most frequently used five broad dimensions to describe the human psyche and personality. The Big Five personality traits are: Conscientiousness, Openness to experience, Extraversion, Agreeableness and Neuroticism. The study conducted by Paulhus and Williams concluded that "Disagreeableness" was the only common Big Five traits of people with the 3 dark personalities. A variety of undesirable human behaviors like aggressiveness, sexual opportunism and impulsivity have an underlying Dark Triad personality. In 2010, psychologists Peter Jonason and Gregory Webster developed the "Dirty Dozen" scale, to identify the potentially troublesome personality traits, with a simple 12-item rating scale. They defined the Dark Triad as a "short-term, agentic, exploitative social strategy", which resonates the fundamentals of Dark Psychology, according to where individuals with woke dark side display violent behavior, in order to fulfil their desires. Now, take a moment and rate each of the 12 items listed below on a 7-point scale and assess where you or someone you know measure up on the "Dirty Dozen" scale:

1. I tend to manipulate others to get my way.

2. I tend to lack remorse.

3. I tend to want others to admire me.

4. I tend to be unconcerned with the morality of my actions.

5. I have used deceit or lied to get my way.

6. I tend to be callous or insensitive.

7. I have used flattery to get my way.

8. I tend to seek prestige or status.

9. I tend to be cynical.

10. I tend to exploit others toward my own end.

11. I tend to expect special favors from others.

12. I want others to pay attention to me.

The total score can range from 12 to 84 and each trait aligns with the specific item on the list as: Narcissism (3, 8, 11, 12); Psychopathy (2, 4, 6, 9); and Machiavellianism (1, 5, 7, 10). According to the study conducted by Webster and Jonason, a score of 45 or more represents high propensity to the Dark Triad personality traits. Don't worry if you score higher than expected cause this scale doesn't capture the subtleties and nuances of a diagnosis, it is as said, a little dirty. The sole purpose of this scale is to provide a quick and easy test, to serve as a warning, if you sense that someone you know might have the Dark Triad traits. We will now explore each of the three Dark Triad traits in details.

Narcissism

The term Narcissism comes from ancient Greek and Roman mythological story, about a handsome hunter named Narcissus who was wandering the world to find someone to love. After rejecting a nymph named Echo, he caught a glimpse of his own reflection in a river, fell in love with it and drowned. This story captured the basic idea of Narcissism, a mental condition marked by elevated and self detrimental involvement, deep need for excessive attention and admiration and a lack of empathy. Narcissists believe themselves to be better looking, more important that anyone else around them and that they deserve special treatment.

Similar to the many characteristics of human psychological traits, Narcissism can be viewed as a spectrum. The two known forms of Narcissism that are also recognized as personality traits are: Grandiose Narcissism and Vulnerable Narcissism. While all Narcissist display an inflated sense of self, Grandiose Narcissists possess an extremely high sense of self-esteem, supreme confidence and no trace of vulnerability. They grow up with an over powering sense of entitlement and abandon situations when they think they are not receiving the respect and admiration that they deserve. Its often noticed that children treated like royalty growing up, with no limitation or hesitation from the parents in meeting their demands, leaves them with an over exaggerated sense of entitlement. Do you know someone who is in a relationship but still looks like they are always on the prowl and make no effort in concealing their desires from their partner or the external world? Such emotionally cold men are referred to as "playboy" and are a classic case of Grandiose Narcissism. They are skilled at hiding their emotions and quickly become dominant and aggressive when others try to meddle in their achievements. These individuals have no regards for thoughts and feelings of others and are ruthless when it comes to fulfilling their desires. According to research studies, individuals with Grandiose Narcissism display significantly positive connection with constructs related to emotional functioning, such as empathy and Emotional Intelligence, but the outcomes of these studies are highly unpredictable and require further verification. It's not surprising that numerous successful politicians and celebrities as well as people on top of their career tend to be Grandiose Narcissist.

On the other hand, Vulnerable Narcissists have very low self-esteem and tendency towards developing a negative view of themselves. People with Vulnerable Narcissism grow up with little to no attention from their parents and are compensating for that neglect by developing an extremely fragile ego, using certain behaviors like self absorption as coping mechanism. These individuals develop deep seated fears of inadequacy and insecurity, with an overwhelming desire for attention and recognition in an attempt to fill that void within. Unlike Grandiose Narcissists, if they do no receive the admiration they think they deserve, the Vulnerable Narcissist will feel emotionally unstable but would not become aggressive and violent. To the Vulnerable Narcissist, the perception that their partner has of them is crucial, but they will still have numerous affairs and not broadcast them owing to their inherent introversion. They are likely to accuse their partners of infidelity and require constant reassurance of their faithfulness. Their need for constant validation, fear of rejection and hypersensitivity to criticism often leaves them feeing anxious and paranoid. They tend to employ child like behaviors such as whining, crying and being overly dramatic to fulfil their demands. Acquiring knowledge and understanding of the type of Narcissist in your life, is the first step in dealing with them successfully.

Bona fide Narcissists or individuals with more extreme form of Narcissism have a mental condition which is marked by an elevated sense of self, deep need for excessive attention and admiration and lack of empathy, which are only serving as a mask for their underlying fragile self esteem that can be easily shaken up by the slightest of the criticism. This psychological condition is called Narcissistic Personality Disorder, affecting 1%-2% of the population and more commonly men. However, this disorder is surrounded by a whole lot of diagnostic confusion due to the high variability of the manifestation of the associated psychological traits. The underlying psychological symptoms are presented with a wide range of severity, from grandiose to self loathing, extraversion to introversion and from being a model citizen to a criminal. This heterogeneity of the symptoms poses a challenge in determining common traits to justify a shared diagnosis. As with more mental disorders, the cause of narcissistic personality disorder is highly complex and remains unknown. It may be linked to our genetics (traits that are inherited), neurobiology (connection between the brain and human behavior) and the environment (excessive adoration or not enough, in the early childhood). Keep in mind, if someone takes too many selfies, it doesn't just make them a Narcissist and there's no clear evidence that social media causes Narcissism. Similarly, children and teens may appear self centered but this may simply be part of their development and doesn't always translate into narcissistic personality disorder.

When the negative traits of narcissistic personality disorder take over people's lives, it causes significant problems like difficult relationships, depression, anxiety, problems at work and even suicidal thoughts or actions. It's like a disease where the patient feels good and the people around them suffer. They tend to act selfishly and narcissistic partners may be dishonest or unfaithful. Narcissism is reported higher in cultures and societies that value individuality and self promotion. Narcissist often fantasize about tremendous power and status as well as being adored and worshipped. They feel it's their birth right to have the respect and admiration that they seek. Their self image is not affected by their actual achievements and circumstances of life. They have an incessant need of attention and flattery regardless of their social behaviors which implicates their outward reality.

Birth of an individual with narcissistic personality disorder in a family of power and status allows for a full and more extreme expression of their Narcissism. For example, Saparmurat Niyazov, leader of Turkmenistan who took over the country filling the power vacuum left behind by the Soviet Union. The total power over a country reached his head and manifested in form of some memorable narcissistic decisions made by him. He ordered renaming the months of the year to reflect his own glory, renaming common household objects in accordance with his whims and eventually declaring himself as the President for Life of Turkmenistan. Hands down the most powerful display of Niyazov's grandiosity was his creation of a religious text that the country had to revere with equal status as that of The Holy Qur'an. A similar evidence can be found in Nazi Germany with their reverence of Hitler's "Mein Kampf" as religious scripture. A more current example of prominent leaders with narcissistic personality disorder would be, North Korean dictator Kim Jong Un, who is afforded the status of holy deities. He had his own uncle assassinated for yawning in one of their meetings, using anti-aircraft weapon.

Machiavellianism

An infamous Italian political philosopher and author of the 16th century, Niccolò Machiavelli, espoused his views on strong leadership, justifying the expense of all moral virtues in lieu of deceit, treachery and manipulation to maintain and gain authority. His most well known work was published as "The Prince", where he wrote "A wise ruler ought never to keep faith when by doing so it would be against his interests," and, "A prince never lacks good reasons to break his promise." By the end of 16th century, dark arts of deception and deceit and the notion that "the end always justifies the means"

in diplomacy became popular as "Machiavellianism". It wasn't until the 1970's, that the social psychologists, Richard Christie and Florence L. Geis, introduced Machiavellianism to modern Psychology and developed "the Machiavellianism Scale" or "The Mach-IV test".

In Psychology, Machiavellianism refers to predisposition of conniving and deceptive traits in individuals that are also inherently master manipulators. Machiavellians are highly strategic in achieving their goals by means of cunning and deceit with a cold heart. They pay little to no attention to emotional damage resulting from their behavior and will use others simply as a stepping stone to reach their goals. This cold mentality of Machiavellians contributes to their aversive and problematic views towards others. The hallmark of this dark trait is constant focus on self-interest, keen understanding of the importance of image and perception with a tendency to ruthlessly exercise power over compassion and mercy. Occasionally the best of us can be duplicitous, like calling in sick when we are well, but Machiavellians routinely cheat and lie in pursuit of their goals.

Over the course of history, many political leaders have resorted to the tactics, ideas and principles from Machiavelli's book "The Prince", as a blueprint for their leadership style. For examples, the political career of Adolf Hitler is the best possible illustration of a Machiavellian leader. Hitler's view that peace should be seen as a brief relief in a never-ending war draws striking resemblance with the views of Machiavelli. He is remembered as a relentless warrior ruler, who desired total control over the entire world under his totalitarian "Third Reich". Hitler was devoted to conquest and manipulated reality to see to his political gains. His false flag operation called "Reichstag Flag" was planned to aid in his predetermined anti communist political agenda of examining and persecuting the Jews. Many parallels can be drawn between Machiavellian's ideology of "ends justify means" and the actual leadership style practiced by Hitler. Being the master manipulator that he was, Hitler successfully manipulated the German political system as well as the hearts and minds of the people. Machiavelli stated "It is better to be feared than loved, if you cannot have both." It's believed that Hitler used to keep a copy of "The Prince" by his bedside. He was adept at triggering responses of love and fear in the German people, that had translated into sheer devotion and even worship.

Machiavelli wrote that "A prince must always seem to be very moral, even if he is not", suggesting that leaders ought to keep a moral appearance but not keep their promises, if their words did not support their best interest. Hitler often delivered exaggerated and hard to implement promises that never came to fruition. He maintained his appearance of a moral leader by creating a perception that he was striving hard to deliver his promises. Machiavelli also argued that making an example of a few offenders is kinder than being overly compassionate, thereby, allowing for chaos to develop in the community. Hitler systematically eliminated any political and social threat to his rise as Germany's leader, by assassinating absolutely anyone who stood in his way and consolidated all the political power to himself.

A brutal and cunning prince of the Papal states, Cesare Borgia, served as a real life model for Machiavelli when writing his book "The Prince". Machiavelli had the front row ticket to the tactics and principles used by Borgia during his reign. Machiavelli visited Borgia to discuss relations with Florence and witnessed the cunning and deceit used by Borgia, to lure his enemies to the city of Senigallia with a promise of friendship, only to have them all assassinated. Borgia died of natural causes at the age of 32 but Machiavelli proceeded to declare that Florence needed a strong leader like Borgia, to unite the people and restore the city's former glory.

Another example of Machiavellian leader would be Joseph Stalin, the ruthless totalitarian dictator of the Soviet Union. He was known to have read and annotated a copy of Machiavellian's book "The Prince". Stalin ordered his military to collect as much grain as possible from the peasants to be used for export in perpetual preparation of war. His launch of "The Great Purge" in 1936, to systematically eliminate opposition to his policies is another usage of Machiavellian tactics. His policies resulted in death of over 20 million Soviet citizens and execution of prominent former party leaders and Leftists, Grigory Zinoviev and Lev Kamenev, on false charges.

Not just political leaders, even business leaders have applied the tactics and ideas of Machiavellianism, as a modern cutthroat approach towards success. One such example is John Gottti, leader of one the most powerful Mafias in the United States. He resorted to use of extreme violence to reach his goals, plotting a murderous coup to seize control of the Gambino Crime Families and assassination his predecessor, Paul Castellano.

Machiavellianism is more prevalent in men than women, however, it can occur in anyone. The golden standard of measuring Machiavellianism is "The Mach-IV test", with 20 different statements such as below that people agree or disagree with:

- "Anyone who completely trusts anyone is asking for trouble."
- "It is safest to assume that all people have a vicious streak, and it will come out when they are given a chance."
- "Most men forget more easily the death of their father than the loss of their property."
- "The biggest difference between most criminals and other people is that the criminals are stupid enough to get caught."

Each statement carries a score of 5 with an overall

score of 100. A score of 60 or above is considered high and those people are called "High Machs", whereas people with scoring below 60 are considered "Low Machs". Below is the graphical representation of how people have scored on the "Mach-IV test".

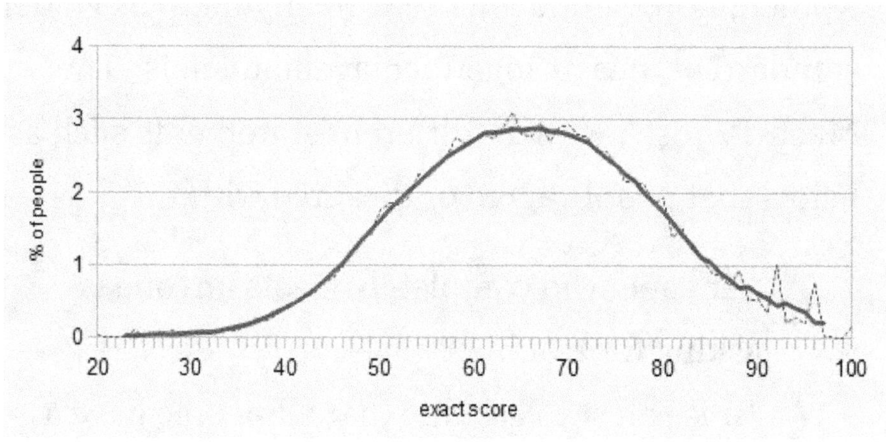

The High Machs are self centered and focus on their own well being. They are enticed by scenarios with ambiguous rules and boundaries. Their cynical outlook and opportunistic nature makes them believe that use of deception and lies are justified to get ahead in life. They are emotionally detached yet friendly and charming in competitive situations.

They fail to see goodness of humanity and mask their true intentions. On the other hand, Low Machs, are more trusting in nature and empathetic towards others. They prefer to play by the rules and their moral compass, believing and expecting most people to do the same. These people avoid manipulation as a means for reaching their goals and are more honest. Individuals scoring too low on the "Mach-IV" scale tend to be submissive, passive and highly agreeable.

In recent times, Machiavellianism has been studied, adapted and applied to businesses and organizations Machiavellianism in the workplace addresses people and business leaders, behaving in a cold and duplicitous manner. Oliver James, published his work on effects of Machiavellianism in the workplace in the book titled: "Office Politics: How to Thrive in a World of Lying, Backstabbing and Dirty Tricks". He proposed a new model of Machiavellianism in business settings consists of three factors: "maintaining power", "harsh management tactics" and "manipulative behaviors". He suggested that success in white-collar environments is driven by office politics. A study conducted on German businesses, revealed that Machiavellianism in an organization can be linked to leadership level and job satisfaction. Another study conducted on people during job interviews, concluded Machiavellian men and women used different tactics to influence the interviewers. High Mach men were more prone to directing the content of the interview and making up information about their job experiences, allowing little to no authority to the interviewer. On the other hand, High Mach women were observed allowing more freedom to the interviewer in directing the content of the interview. Machiavellianism has been shown to positively associate with subordinate perceptions of abusive supervision, a concept dealing with workplace bullying.

Psychopathy

The last and final concept of the unholy trinity of the Dark Triad is Psychopathy. When we hear the word psychopath, we picture a mentally deranged vile looking man who has committed heinous acts of violence, a murderer. But in reality, true psychopaths are more likely to be handsome and charming, with an aura that their prey finds irresistible. Some of the famous Hollywood characters that are etched in our memory, "Patrick Bateman from American Psycho" or "Frank Abagnale Jr. from Catch Me If You Can". These characters were depicted as good looking, intriguing and charming and of course downright terrifying. Psychopathy is often related with people we don't like or understand and construe as evil or a threat to our well being.

Psychopathy is rather difficult to define, but refers to mental disorder when an individual manifests antisocial behaviors, shows no signs of empathy and remorse, expresses extreme egocentricity, lacks the ability to establish meaningful personal relationships masked with superficial charm and impulsivity. Psychopaths exhibit a natural willingness to act in antisocial manner with no significant concern for impact of their behavior on others, suggesting a highly diminished empathic response. Psychopathy is considered as a single personality disorder, however, growing research in this field indicates that Psychopathy is a constellation of multiple Dark Psychology traits. Contradictory with the assumption of being a unified construct, Psychopathy appears to be a complex and multifaceted disorder, marked by amalgamation of different personality traits with a varying degree of reduced inhibition and boldness.

A research study has revealed that Psychopathy is associated with reduced physiological response to perceptual stimuli, even when the individuals imagine themselves to be in threatening situation, suggesting structural abnormalities in their brain. A person's environment, genetic makeup and brain anatomy can contribute to the development or enhancement of the Dark Psychology traits. It's widely perceived that Psychopaths are "born" and not "made, but the overwhelming research suggests that Psychopathy is shaped by varying constitutional causes that are driven by the individual's environment and not just their genetics. The term Psychopathology refers to combination of individual's genes and environmental influences causing impaired functioning of psychological and neurological processes and expression of Psychopathic traits.

Another research study indicates that Psychopathic traits are genetically selected because of their increased value in reproductive success for certain individuals in some specific ancestral environments. This can be observed with high propensity of Psychopaths to have multiple short term sexual relationships and exploitative behaviors like rape, infidelity and violence. They can easily manipulate their prey or coerce them into fulfilling their sexual desires. Psychopaths appear confident and self assured with concealed cunning motivations masked with deception and convincing lies. Just as callous as Machiavellians, Psychopaths tend to be more reckless and impulsive. For example, the story of Ted Bundy is that of a textbook Psychopathic killer on the loose. He was a master of deception and was able to deceive people not just physically but also psychologically. All his victims had a fatal attraction towards him and found him to be charming and desirable moments before he brutally murdered them in cold blood, hallmark signs of a

Psychopath. Bundy was also a Narcissist, who often referred to himself in third person and was completely emotionally detached from the consequences of his antisocial behaviors on others.

In 1944, Psychologist John Bowlby conducted a research study on adolescent juvenile delinquents in a child guidance clinic. Bowlby proposed that a person's disturbed mental health and behavioral problems could be traced back to a troubled childhood. He believed that the first five years of a mother and infant's relationship contributed significantly to the social skills of the child and any disruption of this relationship could lead to antisocial behavior or psychopathy. Bowlby selected 88 children from the guidance clinic, of these 44 were juvenile thieves and the other 44 children, had emotional problems but had not committed any crimes, were used as control group for his study. Several tests and interviews were conducted on children and their parents. The results indicated that more than 50% of the delinquents had been separated from their mothers for over six months during their infancy and only 2 such cases were found in the control group. Bowlby found that 14 of the juvenile thieves were unable to feel affection for or care about others, displaying what he called as "affectionless psychopathy", as depicted in the picture below. None of the children from the control group showed any such signs. He concluded that maternal separation or depravation in the first five years of development led to permanent emotional damage, characterized by inability to form long meaningful relationship.

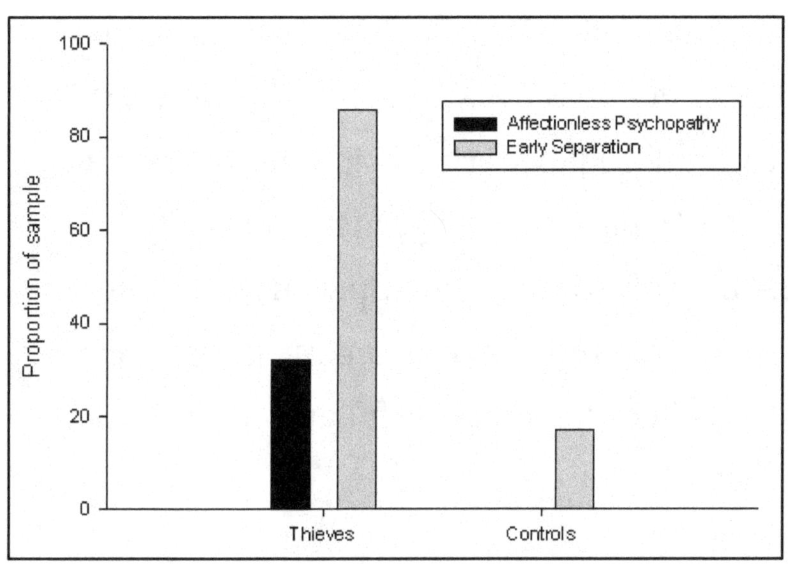

Bowlby postulated that humans are born with innate behaviors called "social releasers" such as crying and smiling, to aid proximity and contact with their mother. The emotional attachment and relationship of a mother and her child acts as a base model based on which all future social relationships are formed. According to "Bowlby's Maternal Deprivation Hypothesis", any long term disruption of the relationship between mother and infant results in antisocial behaviors, delinquency, depression, increased aggressiveness, cognitive difficulties and affectionless psychopathy. An intriguing example of affectionless psychopath would be Andy McNab, who was abandoned as a baby, committed petty crimes, joined the British Army Infantry at a young age and eventually became part of Britain's elite Special Air Services (SAS) unit. Post retirement from his military career, McNab has become a successful author and playwright.

Professor Kevin Dutton from University of Oxford, collaborated with McNab on the book titled "The Good Psychopath's Guide to Success", suggesting that psychopathic traits could be made useful given the circumstances. Dutton is a leading psychological research at the Department of Experimental Psychology and a member of "Oxford Centre for Emotions and Affective Neuroscience (OCEAN)" research group. McNab is a diagnosed psychopath but Dutton purported that McNab was able to selectively control his psychopathic traits to consciously take advantage of the situation at hand. He could dial up his fearlessness and empathy or dial down ruthlessness and impulsivity, to get the best out of himself and others in a wide variety of situations, claiming the title of "good psychopath". Dutton is on the record saying: "I'd done research with the special forces, with surgeons, with top hedge fund managers and barristers. Almost all of them had psychopathic traits, but they'd harnessed them in ways to make them better at what they do." Unlike most people, psychopaths make some of the best operators in high pressure situations, like terror attacks or kidnapping, owing to their fearlessness and ability to focus solely on the job at hand and blocking out the white noise. Dutton's work is considered revolutionary as it explores the positive implications of Dark Psychology, that is traditionally maligned.

In 2011, Dutton conducted "Great British Psychopathic Survey" and identified professions with higher likelihood of a psychopathic leader, such as lawyers, police officers, journalists and surgeons among other professions requiring extensive professional detachment. For example, CEOs of hedge funds are often required to make high risk decisions with little to no fear, hallmark trait of psychopathy which can be dialed up by the so called "good psychopaths", to make millions of dollars.

People often use the terms "sociopath" and psychopath interchangeably, however, sociopath is a nonclinical term and refers strictly to people with antisocial behaviors primarily driven by their environmental factors. On the other hand, psychopathic traits have a genetic predisposition, exasperated by their environment. Sociopaths often exhibit Antisocial Personality Disorder (ASPD), characterized by low empathy and moral check. Unlike Psychopathy, the *Diagnostic and Statistical Manual of Mental Disorders* (5th edition), includes ASPD as a personality disorder. Individuals diagnosed with ASPD have a history of another mental health condition called "conduct disorder" at an early age, characterized by failure to abide by laws and follow norms, leading to criminal behaviors. ASPD is solely dependent and focused on social behavior of the subject, while Psychopathy is a diagnosis driven by multiple psychopathic personality traits.

Similar to the other two personality disorders of the Dark Triad, Psychopathy is a spectrum disorder and can be diagnosed using 20 item symptom rating scale, developed by Canadian psychologist Robert Hare in 1970s. The "Hare Psychopathy Checklist", now the "Psychopathy Checklist- revised (PCL-R)" is a diagnostic tool to assess the presence of psychopathy and antisocial tendencies in people for clinical, research or legal purposes. Today PCL-R test is frequently used in courtroom as an indicator of the potential risk posed by the accused or prisoner and in determination of the length and type of sentences and treatments of the subjects in light of forensic evidences.

The Hare PCL-R test has 2 different components, a review of the person's history and a semi structured interview. The true assessment can only be carried out by psychology or mental health professionals. The clinician will evaluate and score 20 items on the checklist, covering traits like: "glib and superficial charm", "grandiose (exaggeratedly high) estimation of self", "need for stimulation", "pathological lying", "cunning and manipulativeness", "lack of remorse or guilt", "shallow affect (superficial emotional responsiveness)", "callousness and lack of empathy", "parasitic lifestyle", "poor behavioral controls", "sexual promiscuity", "early behavior problems", "lack of realistic long-term goals". The other part of the diagnosis would be an interview covering subject's detailed background and history. Each of the twenty items are scored from 0-2 based on the subject's responses, with a maximum score of 40 depicting prototypical psychopath. People with a score of 30 or above are diagnosed as clinical psychopaths. Subjects with no criminal background normally scored around 5 while many non-psychopathic criminal offenders reported an average score of 22. To put this scale in perspective; notorious serial killers, Ted Bundy and Peter Lundin, scored 39/40 on their PCL-R test.

A complete understanding of the Dark Triad requires a brief overview of the concept of "Sadism". The "Sadistic Personality Disorder" has been proposed by an increasing majority of modern day psychologists as the fourth pillar of the Dark Triad or the new Dark Tetrad. Most of us find it next to impossible to relate with Sadism as a personality trait, posing a challenge in gaining an understanding of this concept as part of the Dark Psychology. Unlike Narcissism, Machiavellianism, and Psychopathy, people often alienate Sadism failing to recognize and acknowledge the signs and expression of this disorder. In layman terms, Sadism refers to mental condition where the subject derives joy and pleasure solely from the sufferings of other people. Addition of Sadism to any of the three personality disorders of the Dark Triad individually leads to mind boggling manifestation of criminal behavior. For example, Machiavellian leader may inflict pain on his empire just to derive pleasure from their suffering with no substantial gains. The occurrence of Sadism cannot be credited to an inherent lack of self control and is a voluntary act of criminal intent. Sadism is downright cruelty on people viewed as a means of entertainment or sport. A host of sexual fantasies, urges and behaviors that are outside the norm, can potentially manifest as causing harm and distress to the partner, especially in cases without consent. This disorder is one of the many psychiatric sexual disorders categorized as "paraphilic" disorder called "Sexual Sadism" disorder. People with Sexual Sadism cause physical pain and humiliation to achieve sexual gratification. These sexual sadistic acts may include spanking, biting, whipping or physical bondages like handcuffs and ropes. Remember, if these acts are played out with a consenting adult, causing no physical or mental distress or dysfunction, then it would not be

considered a disorder. However, extreme Sexual
Sadism that leads to serious danger and harm to the
other person or death is criminal. The psychotic
traits of Dark Psychology like lack of empathy and
remorse, impulsivity, ruthlessness and deceit can
render Sadism especially dangerous and an
anathema for the society.

Chapter 5: Neuro-Linguistic Programming (NLP)

In the 1970s, psychological researcher John Grinder, coined the term Neuro-Linguistic Programming (NLP) for a mind controlling method to change our conscious thoughts and behaviors as desired. Neuro (mind/information) Linguistic (language/words) Programming (learning/control), simply put it's the art of learning the language of your mind to generate satisfying results. NLP is a lot like a User Manual for the brain, to help you communicate the goals and desires of the unconscious mind to the conscious self. Imagine you are in foreign country and craving chicken wings, so you go to a restaurant to order the same but when the food shows up, it ends up being liver stew because of a failed communication. Humans often fail to recognize and acknowledge their unconscious thoughts and desires because a lot of it gets lost in translation to the conscious self. NLP enthusiasts often exclaim: "the conscious mind is the goal setter, and the unconscious mind is the goal getter". The idea being your unconscious mind wants you to achieve everything that you actually desire but if your conscious mind fails to receive the message, you will never set the goal to achieve those dreams.

NLP was developed using excellent therapists and communicators who had achieved great successes as role models. It's a set of tool and techniques to help your master communication, both with yourself and others. NLP is study of human mind combining thoughts and actions with perception to fulfil their deepest desires. Our mind employs complex neural networks to process information and use language or auditory signals to give it meaning while storing these signals in patterns to generate and store new memories. We can voluntarily use and apply certain tools and techniques to alter our thoughts and actions in achieving our goals. These techniques can be perceptual, behavioral and communicative and used control our own mind as well as that of others.

One of the central ideas of NLP is that our conscious mind has a bias towards a specific sensory system called the "Preferred Representational System (PRS)". Phrases like "I hear you" or "Sounds good" signal an auditory PRS, whereas, phrase like "I see you" may signal a visual PRS. A certified therapist can identify a person's PRS and model their therapeutic treatment around it. This therapeutic framework often involves rapport building, goal setting and information gathering among other activities. NLP is increasingly used by individuals to promote self enhancement, such as self reflection and confidence as well as for social skill development, primarily communication.

NLP therapy or training can be delivered in the form of language and sensory based interventions, using behavior modification techniques customized for individuals to better their social communication and improved confidence and self awareness. NLP therapists or trainers strive to make their client understand that their view and perception of the world is directly associated with how they operate in it, and the first step toward a better future is keen understanding of their conscious self and contact with their unconscious mind. Its paramount to first analysis and subsequently change our thoughts and behaviors that are counterproductive and block our success and healing. NLP has been successfully used in treatment of various mental health conditions like anxiety, phobias, stress and even post traumatic stress disorder. An increasing number of practitioners are commercially applying NLP to promise improved productivity and achievement of work oriented goals that ultimately lead to job progression.

Now, let's look at how NLP works. John Grinder, in association with his student Richard Bandler, conducted a research study on techniques used by Fritz Perls (founder of Gestalt therapy), Virginia Satir (Family therapist) and Milton Erickson (renowned Hypnotherapist). They subsequently analyzed and streamlined these therapy techniques to create a behavioral model for mass application in order to achieve sand reproduce excellence in any field. Bandler, a computer science major, helped develop a "psychological programming language" for human beings. On the basis of how our mind processes information or perceives the external world, it generates an internal "NLP map" of what is going on outside. This internal map is created based on the feedback provided by our sense organs, like the pictures we take in, sounds we hear, the taste in our mount, sensations we feel on our skin and what we can smell. However, with this massive influx of information, our mind selectively deletes and generalizes a ton of information. This selection is unique to every person and is determined by what our mind deems relevant to our situation. As a result, we often miss out on a whole lot of information that can be immediately noticed by someone else right off the bat and we end up with a tiny and skewed version of what is really occurring. For example, take a moment and process this statement: "Person A killed person B", now depending on our circumstances and experiences we will all have our own version of that story. Some might think a "a man killed a woman", or "a lion killed a man" or "a terrorist killed a baby" or "John Doe killed Kennedy" and so on and so forth. Now, there's a method to this madness, whatever story you came up with, realize there is way you got to that story which was driven by our own life experience. Our mind creates an internal map of the situation at hand and then we compare that map with other internal maps from our past that we have stored in our mind. Every person has their own internal "library" based on what is important or relevant to them in accordance with their personality. Once the mind settles with a preexisting mental map that is comparable to the new one, it starts adding meaning to what is happening and decides how you feel about it and ultimately your response to it. Your physical and mental state has a significant impact on the meaning that your mind makes from moment to moment. Whether you are physically sick, or emotionally stressed or even happy and relaxed can alter how you add meaning to the situations. For instance, the physical sensations of terror and excitement are the same, like increased heart rate, high blood pressure and even palpitations, so the meaning that our mind adds to these sensations decides whether we are just ecstatic or terrorized. It always comes down to the story that you write in your mind.

"The laws that apply to mechanical, non living systems are not the same laws that apply to the interaction of biological, living systems." – John Grinder

Did you ever feel that once your conscious mind makes you aware of what you want to do or gain, suddenly the universe seems to be propping up signs that could help you find your way to get what you want? For example, one day you wake up thinking I need to take my family on a vacation. You go on with your day the same way as you have been for days or weeks, but you suddenly notice a poster on an exciting trip to Florida on your way to work, that you later learnt from your coworker has been up for over a month now. You suddenly see that close to that same Starbucks you visit every day, there is a big travel agency that you had never paid attention to. When browsing the Internet, you will suddenly see travel ads all over your Facebook or ads from Airbnb popping up on your YouTube videos. Now all these may come across as coincidences, but the matter of the fact is those things or signs had been there all along but your mind deleted that information or perception because they were not relevant to you. So as your conscious mind starts connecting the dots between your wishes and the reality of the world, you start picking up on new information that may have already been in plain sight, but you are only tuned into now.

Your personality profile also plays a major role in what information your mind chooses to exclude and what is processed. People who are more focused on security, they are constantly assessing their situation to determine whether its safe for you or not. On the other hand, people who are more freedom oriented, they tend to think of their situation in terms of options and limitation with no focus on safety at all. Your personality determines what and how you update your mental library and ultimately the meaning you add to these internal maps. For example, a kid looking at a roller coaster is thinking only about the fun of traveling through open space in a cool looking ride and given the opportunity will easily and fearlessly jump on the ride, because his personality is not security oriented. But an adult who is able to focus not only on the fun and excitement of the ride but also it's safety and potential hazards, will think twice before making that same decision.

Bottom line is "We respond to our Map of reality, not the reality itself" and all meaning is open to unique interpretation by each one of us. The light at the end of tunnel is that with NLP, you can control your reality, so if there is something you don't like or the way it makes you feel, YOU CAN CHANGE IT!

"The only justification for the application of NLP patterns, is the creation of choice, in precisely those sets of context in which the choice presently does not exist." - John Grinder

Here are some prominently used NLP techniques:

- **Anchoring**

    A Russian scientist, Ivan Pavlov, conducted an experiment on dogs by repeatedly ringing a bell while the dogs were eating and concluded that he could get the dogs to salivate by the ringing the bell anytime, even when there was no food present. This neurobiological connection observed in the dogs, between the bell and salivation is called a conditioned response or "anchor". Thus, the process of creating a perceivable sensory trigger to the state of how you feel is called Anchoring.

    Try this yourself! Think of a gesture or sensation on your body (pulling your earlobe, cracking your knuckles, or touching your forehead) and associate it with any desired positive emotional response (happiness, confidence, calmness etc.) by recalling and reliving the memory when you actually experienced those emotions. The next time you are feeling stressed or low, you can trigger this anchor voluntarily and you will notice your feeling will immediately change. To strengthen triggered response, you can think of another memory when your felt the desired emotion and relive it. Every time you add a new memory to the mix, your anchor will become more potent and trigger a stronger response.

- **Content Reframing**

  This NLP technique is best suited to combat negative thoughts and feelings. With the use of this visualization techniques you can alter your mind to think differently about situations where you feel threatened or disempowered. Simply view the negative situation and reframe it's meaning into something positive. For example, let's say you just broke up with your long term girlfriend or boyfriend. You will most likely be hurt and in pain. But you can choose to reframe the end of your relationship with empowering thoughts of being single and new potential relationships. You can choose to focus on the lessons you learnt from your past relationship and how you can implement them to have an even better relationship in future. Thus, by simply reframing the break up, you can feel better and empower yourself.

This technique has massive appeal in treatment of post traumatic stress disorder and for people who have experienced child abuse or are suffering from chronic or life threatening diseases.

- **Rapport Building**

    Rapport is the art of generating empathy in others by pacing and mirroring their verbal and non-verbal behaviors. People like other people who they think are similar to themselves. When you can subtly mirror the other person, their brain will fire off "mirror neurons" or "pleasure sensors" in their brain, which make them feel a sense of liking for you. You can simply stand or sit the way the other person or tilt your head in the same direction as theirs or the best of all, just smile when they smile. All these cues will help you build rapport with the other person. The social significance of rapport building cannot be underscored. Strong personal and professional connections lead to a happier and longer life.

- **Dissociation**

  The NLP technique of dissociation guides you in severing the link between negative emotions and the associated trigger. For instance, certain words or phrases may instantly bring back bad memories and make you feel stressed or depressed. If you can successfully identify those triggers and make an effort to detach those negative feelings from it, you are one step closer to healing and empowering yourself. A slew of mental health conditions like anxiety, depression and even phobias can be effectively treated with this technique. It can also be used to positively deal with difficult situations at home and work.

- **Future Pacing**

  The NLP technique of leading the subject to a future state and rehearsing the potential future outcomes so as to achieve the desired outcome automatically, is called

Future Pacing. It's a type of visualization technique or mental imagery, used to anchor a change or resources to future situations by imagining and virtually experiencing those situations. A skilled manipulator can lead their victim on a mental journey into the future and influence the responses occurring when the future unfolds. An expert NLP user with prominent Dark Psychological traits may cognitively transport their victim into the future and suggest outcomes while monitoring the victim's response to eventually get their own desired outcome into the psyche of the victim.

- **Influence and Persuasion**

  This is definitely the most ambivalent NLP technique and houses a gray area between Dark Psychology and Psychotherapy. NLP is primarily focused on eliminating negative emotions, curb bad habits and resolve conflicts, another aspect of NLP deals with ethically influencing and persuade others. Now pay attention to the word ETHICAL here.

One of the prominent psychology therapist to participate in Grinder's original research on NLP was, Milton Erickson, leading hypnotherapist and founder of the "American Society for Clinical Hypnosis". Erickson was so adept at hypnosis that he could literally hypnotize anyone anywhere and communicate with people's subconscious mind without needing hypnosis. He helped construct the "Milton Model" of NLP, designed to induce trance like state in people, using abstract language patterns. According to the Milton Model, using artfully vague and deliberately ambiguous sentences will trigger the person to search for meaning of what they hear from their own life experiences and fill in the details subconsciously. This powerful tool can be used to not only ethically influence and persuade people but also help people deal with some deep seated negative emotions, overcome fears and increase their self awareness.

Hypnosis is the perfect segue to the use of NLP in the Dark Psychology. When most people think of the word "hypnotism", they picture an old guy with moustache and a top hat, waving his pocket watch at someone and telling them they are about to fall asleep. This is more of a movie version of hypnotism to let the audience know that hypnotism means you give someone else total control of your mind. The real hypnotists are out there and can easily draw upon the darkest psychological traits to influence and persuade people to their own advantage. The dark hypnotists victimize people in their vulnerable state by making deep, impactful suggestions and developing a high level of power over them. The suggestions are made with subtlety and nearly impossible to be detected by the victim. By definition, hypnosis gives access to the deepest and unconscious mind of the victim. A skilled hypnotist can make you give them the key to your mental library, rip you off emotionally and even replace your thoughts and feelings with that of his own, without raising any alarms or giving you an opportunity to protect yourself.

From a bird's eye view, hypnotism can occur with verbal and non verbal cues. Or suggestions. The dark hypnotist makes a decision regarding which tactic they deem as best suited for their victim in given situation. And some might just utilize the technique they find the most amusing in playing with their victim's psyche. Verbal suggestion can be hard to detect since dark hypnotists can actually use words that sound similar or more common innocent words. For example, a dark hypnotist attempting to instill suicidal thoughts and feelings in their victim, will use words like "You want to dine" to conceal the underlying command of "You want to die". They could bring up an upcoming plan and say "Remember that restaurant by the hill, you want to die, somewhere that is popular and scenic" and the victim's subconscious mind will absorb that suggestion of death with no conscious rationale. At the off chance that someone picked up on the true words of the hypnotist, imagine how crazy they would come across calling them out. Human psyche always chooses the psychologically easier option and will therefore simply accept the deceptive command with no reasoning.

Another tactic employed by the dark hypnotists is altering the tone of their voice and carefully choosing their sentences. This is where rapport building with their victim comes in handy. The dark hypnotist will would carefully observe the speed and style of delivery used by their victim while expressing serious thoughts. For example, someone might use low pitch and slow pace while saying something of grave importance to them, the observing dark hypnotist will make a mental not of this information and proceed to make verbal suggestions in that exact tone of their own voice. This mirrored tone of voice with careful modulation, will deliver the intended message into the subconscious mind of the victim, penetrating all of the victim's defenses and then switch back to their usual tone to avoid any detection by the victim. Shifting the gear back to the words or phrases used by the dark hypnotist into succumbing their victims. They study their victim and pick on words that have special significance for the victim. Similar to the unique tone of voice we all use when sharing meaningful thoughts, each one of us also possesses a list of personal words of meaning that we relate with these serious thoughts. These words further enhance the grasp of the dark hypnotists on their victims, allowing the hypnotist to reverse engineer the victim's mind and use it against themselves.

As mentioned earlier, the dark hypnotist can also use non verbal suggestions and use manipulative body language to gain control over the victim. As powerful as our mind can be, it is susceptible to the smallest of physical cues. Even political leaders have reported to have changed their hairstyle to alter the intention while delivering high profile speeches. The whole idea revolves around association of external stimuli with strong emotional responses. For example, a dark hypnotist may move their eyes in the same way as the victim did while experiencing panic to trigger a feeling of panic in the victim. The victim would subconsciously link the eye movement to the feeling of panic. The other key non verbal suggestion used by the dark hypnotists is the environmental stimulus. Think of the principal's office as a child when being reprimanded for your disorderly conduct. We subconsciously associate the principal's office with feeling of panic so we built a connection between the physical location and feeling experienced at that location. Hypnotists will plan to carry out specific conversation at specific location only. For example, if the hypnotist was in a romantic relationship with someone, they will take their victim to the same coffee shop every time they are looking to get consent or agreement from the victim. Over time, victim begins to associate the coffee shop as place for granting permission to their "lover".

A deep insight into the Dark Psychology of NLP is provided by the case study of of of NLP's co-creator, Richard Bandler. He serves as a textbook example of how users of Dark Psychology can successfully create a false public image while tactfully concealing the harsh reality. Let's deep dive into this paradox. Bandler boasts a long list of therapeutic achievements, such as overcoming his handicap of wheel chair and curing schizophrenic patients using unconventional methods that were out right dismissed by the mainstream Psychology. These achievements helped Bandler build and partially maintain, a public image of mild mannered, grandfather like person who exudes positivity, which is far from the truth. In reality Bandler is a heavy drug (cocaine) user and charged with murder of a woman, although found not guilty. Bandler lives in violation of his own claims of the power of NLP in addressing a person's mental health conditions. During Bandler's murder trial, prosecutors provided concrete evidence that the woman was shot using Bandler's gun and Bandler testified that the gun was used by his cocaine dealer and not by Bandler himself. While recalling his trial, Bandler is more likely to surpass the gravity of the incidence and comment on the time taken by the jury on his acquittal. Bandler was confronted over his drug use, during his trial, and he plainly stated that he had an addiction to unhealthy foods like candy and peanuts, which he insisted were actually worse for his health than cocaine. Think about it, Bandler used the reframing NLP technique to convert a rather grave situation into a lighthearted and rational situation that resonates with a lot of people. Even when discussing death of someone Bandler knew, he is able to compare cocaine with candy and peanuts. This goes to show how skilled hypnotists and NLP users, are able to control the selective focus of their victims to their advantage.

Next time you feel threatened or believe someone is trying to control or manipulate you, use these tips to recognize and deal with NLP users:

- Be wary of people mirroring your body language. If you notice someone you have discussed NLP with, copying your gestures or the way you sit. Let them know that you are on to them.
- Move your eyes randomly to throw off the NLP user, who may be keenly observing your eye movement and pretending to be intensely interested in what you are saying.
- Ward off potential anchoring, by not allowing the NLP user to touch you during your heightened state of emotion.
- Don't buy into permissive language used and vague statements made by the NLP user, who is attempting to induce a trance like state in you.

- Pay attention to the statements made by the NLP user, who may use similar sounding innocent words to manipulate your unconscious mind.

- Most importantly be self aware and trust your intuition!

Chapter 6: Undetected Mind Control

An innate need for mankind is to feel that we are in total control of our self, believing that we have a safe space inside our mind where we can have private thoughts that are inaccessible to the outside world. Our mind is our sanctuary! Consider the fact that when you are dreaming, you are never in control of what happens next. When you are trying to get through that assignment, are you able to control your mind from wandering? Our minds are extremely powerful and able to process completely distinct thoughts in the same moment at an unparalleled speed but at the same time our thoughts can be easily influences by external factors. For example, when you are watching a movie, your mind and emotions are influenced and even led by what's happening on the screen, the music being played and even the camera work. Your brain responds to the cues it picks up on even though you are consciously aware that you are just watching a movie and no one is trying to kill you with a machete. If our mind can be influenced by prompts we have chosen ourselves and are aware of, the influence being exerted by a skilled dark psychological manipulators could easily be dangerously strong.

As is consistent with the dark pattern of predatory behavior of people with active Dark Psychology, the undetected mind controllers also exhibit the desire to influence the prey for their own benefits. Undetected mind controllers are highly logical and are likely to act only after carefully assessing the situation and the state of their victim. However, unlike other manipulators they tend to be more cowardly. The art of mind control is no easy endeavor to begin with but trying to keep your motive hidden through the process is like climbing the Himalayas on a cold breezy night. The undetected mind controller has to be patient and cunning and carefully study their target and use all that knowledge about the victim to their own detriment. They are as afraid of being caught in their action as a deer drinking water at the ravine is afraid of being pounced by the tiger lurking in the bushes.

In reference to undetected mind control, we are talking about situations where the victim fails to recognize and acknowledge that their thoughts and feelings are being influenced by the external stimuli presented by the manipulator. This unawareness prevents the victim from defending themselves verbally, physically and mentally. The victim is unable to exercise control in the situation or even bring his "fight or flight" reflex in action, leaving them highly vulnerable. To be able to put our defenses up in time, our mind needs to be able to detect the threat.

At a very high level, undetected mind control techniques can be categorized into two: interpersonal interactions and the use of mass media. Some research studies have suggested that a handful of dominant institutions are exerting power to affect how you think, act or feel, without us ever noticing it. The conventional media mind control tactics were reserved for the large companies but with advent of modern electronic gadgets and readily accessible internet, media mind control tactics are increasing used by the dark manipulators.

For those of you who have watched the famous TV show, "Mad Men", you are probably familiar with the 1960's world of advertising on Madison Avenue and of course, the genius workings of the top ad man, "Don Draper". What if I told you there actually was a "Don Draper" in the real world? In the early 19th century, Edward Bernays, nephew of Sigmund Freud, was deemed as "the father of public relations". Bernays successfully applied the insights he received from his uncle on the subconscious human mind to develop his own methods of mind control, creating the modern day American consumer. Bernays was quick to realize that public opinion, thoughts, attitude and behaviors could be studied and highly malleable. For example, with the turn of the century and industrial revolution, cigars could be made by machines. The traditional cigar smoker sought pride in his authentic hand rolled cigars. So to promote a brand of cigar that was made by machine, Bernays campaigned against the adverse health effects of someone else's spit and distributed 30,000 anti-spit warnings. He changed the focus of the cigar smokers from the authenticity of cigar to how it was being produced, creating the environment where his product seemed like the natural choice.

Another example of Bernay's genius of controlling the public mind set to benefit his product is the American luggage industry. In 1920s, massive decline in sale of luggage and increasing preference for small luggage was rather alarming to the luggage industry so they turned to Bernays to pull them out of the deep end. In response, Bernays sent articles to popular women magazines highlighting the need for women to travel with a versatile wardrobe and appropriate clothing for various activities. He encouraged store owners to display luggage in their windows to establish a link between new clothes and new luggage styles. He even created the "Luggage Information Service" and lobbied to increase the free weight allowance on airplanes. Sounds a lot like the cunning of "Don Dapper", right? In 1934, green became the color of the chic fashion statement. How? Thanks to the ad campaign run by Bernays for the cigarette company called "The Lucky Strikes". Ding,ding,ding...your "Mad Men" recollection is spot on! When George Washington

Hill, owner of "Lucky Strikes" refused to change the appearance of the box of his cigarettes from "big red bull's eye on green backdrop" to more neutral colors, that Bernays had suggested would coordinate more with people's clothing, Bernays decided to make the color green fashionable. Few of the tactics he used in his campaign are: encouraging artists and psychologists to discuss the color green; organized a "Color Fashion Bureau"; sent 1500 letters to interior decorators, club women, and home furniture buyers on green letter-headed paper; convinced the President of "Onondaga Silk Company" to have green menus for his lunch event for magazine editors, and to serve green food.

"Emphasis by repetition gains acceptance for an idea, particularly if the repetition comes from different sources." – Edward Bernays

The use of mass media in promoting desires and status symbols plays a pivotal role in our capitalist ecosystem. Human mind has evolved to process visual signals far more powerfully than the signals received by any of our other 4 senses. When we remember someone, we quickly visualize their picture rather than associating any other sensory input with them. As they say, "A picture is worth a thousand words". Traditionally, the usage of mass media was confined in the hands of institutions or companies to ethically sway public opinion. What has changed though, is the use of burgeoning technology of social media, by the new generation of mind controllers, to penetrate the minds of innocent people, even deeper than what our forebears could deem possible. The contemporary interfaces of our new daily routines are the sound of a new text message on our smartphones and the number of "likes" and "thumbs-up" emoji on our posts or pictures telling us how popular we are. Our mind subconsciously turns on behavioral loops in the presence of these external stimuli, known as "hot triggers". These sources of instant gratification turn us into the rats on a wheel, always wanting to go back for more. Think about it, started in a dorm room, "Facebook" has grown into a multi billion-dollar company with over 1.5 billion active users worldwide.

It's growing public knowledge, that Internet has an underground "Dark Web" where individuals with Dark Psychological Traits are watching the world in search of their next prey. The fact that Facebook has been involved in numerous controversies from the 2016 Presidential Election of America, concerning the spread of biased and false rhetoric undermining the American democracy is alarming. As a matter of fact, Facebook conducted a research on its mass penetration and influence on the American people, by sending a "Go Out & Vote" notifications to over 60 million users on the 2010 Presidential election day. They reported positive outcome from over 340k who were unlikely to vote without the Facebook reminder. Now if Facebook selectively sent the notifications to the supporter of a particular party, they could potentially flip the election results without coming under the radar. Another controversial experiment carried out by Facebook was manipulation of the emotional state of over 600k users by sending them excessive positive or negative words on their new feeds.

The undetected mind control is not restricted to just the social media platforms. Most people assume that when they use online search engines like Google, Yahoo or Bing, they are carefully conducting research on a particular topic but the reality is than 90% of our views are on the top ten links presented to us by the search engine. Sure Google produces thousands of web pages containing our search phrase but its underlying algorithm also prioritizes the results for us and influence what most of us will learn about our topic. Psychologist Robert Epstein, called this phenomenon as "Search Engine Manipulation Effect". Epstein conducted an experiment to assess whether the "Search Engine Manipulation Effect" could impact how people cast their vote in an election. He asked three groups of

Americans to research candidates for an Australian election, using his own mock search engine, served up the same search results to each group but changed the order in which the results were presented. He created a bias for each group to favor one candidate over the other. The results showed 48% increase in each group for the search engine's "favored" candidate, confirming the validity of the "Search Engine Manipulation Effect". Unethical hackers with dark psychological traits can easily use these web technologies to exert mind control on their prey and never get caught.

The other prominent tactic used for undetected mind control is interpersonal interactions. It is scientifically proven that an individual with a pressing need or desire tends to be more susceptible and vulnerable to undetected mind control. The need could be as simple as wanting water to quench your thirst or as complex as search for love and affection. For instance, when you are looking for a specific person in a crowd, like your new crush at the gym, your mind manages to screen and filter out all the people in the background and immediately hone in on that one person. This happens because once our brain recognizes what you desire, it is able to direct us toward it without us even realizing it. This phenomenon is also called "Subliminal Influence" and the term is used interchangeably with undetected mind control. The skilled mind controller can discreetly figure out what their victim's goals are and manipulate their prey with that information.

An experiment conducted on subliminal influence, studies two sets of people, one set was thirsty and other set was not. Both sets were shown a film with a hidden image of an iced tea. They were then allowed to purchase a drink from the wide selection of beverages. The people from the thirsty set purchased iced tea in greater numbers than statistically expected. This goes to show that when a person's mind is desperate for something, it is more open to suggestions. If a dark mind controller finds a victim yearning for some deep emotional need, the manipulator will have greater ease at controlling their mind. For example, an individual who recently suffered a breakup and is craving company encounters a mind controller, they will easily influence the victim into thinking that they are the victim's savior when, in reality, they are the predator. Some real life vulnerabilities that dark mind controllers seek in their victims are: their need for financial stability, their need for belonging, and their need for love. The dark mind controller may seek to sexually or financially abuse their victim, gain their allegiance to some form of cult or simply play with the victim for their own sadistic pleasure.

"Mind control is a process by which individual or collective freedom of choice and action is compromised by agents or agencies that modify or distort perception, motivation, affect, cognition and/or behavioral outcomes" – Philip Zimbardo

If you ask people if they are familiar with mind control, they will probably tell you that they are indeed familiar with "Brainwashing". In the 1950s, American journalist Edward Hunter had first used the term brainwashing, in his report n the treatment of American troops in Chinese prison camps during the "Korean War". More people are aware of brainwashing than mind control and they mistake their vague familiarity with the concept of brainwashing for accurate understanding. Psychologist Steve Hassan, made a key distinction between mind control and brainwashing, stating "In brainwashing, the victim knows that the aggressor is an enemy". For example, prisoners of war often choose to change their belief system, even when they are aware that the brainwashing is behind done by the enemy, as a resort to stay alive. However, when the prisoners are able to escape the enemy, the effects of the brainwashing disappear. Unlike brainwashing, mind control is subtle and often the manipulator is considered a friend, so the victim never even tries to defend themselves and acts as a "willing" participant. A majority of the Dark Psychology techniques are like sniper bullets and directed at one particular person at a time, whereas brainwashing is like an atomic bomb, capable causing mass destruction in a second.

Brainwashing can turn otherwise innocent people into suicide bombers and terrorists. Brainwashing refers to the slow process of gradually replacing an individual's ideas, beliefs and mental identity with that of the brainwasher. This technique can be used to control an individual or a whole country. The brainwashing techniques have been tried and tested and proved to be working effectively in any imaginable situation. For example, members of cults are widely thought of as victims of brainwashing but most people fail to explain what a cult is and how they brainwash their recruits. A cult is a "fringe group of people showing intense devotion to a particular cause, person, or work". The charismatic cult leader is able to exert high influence over his followers, who blindly follow the leader's preaching. The main attraction of cults is presentation of simple, achievable reality for those who are willing to embrace cult's teachings. The fast paced modern world can be overwhelming and rather confusing for a lot of us. Cults manage to cut through this confusion and prey on our need for belonging and acceptance. The ideological brainwashing of cults is enforced by persistent social reinforcement of the cult's teachings. Cults are a lot like drug dealers, pouncing on the first high sought by the victim of their own volition. This initial search and readiness of the victims make them highly susceptible to the brainwashing itself.

When brainwashing is based on an ideology and not an individual, the stakes are even higher. A perfect example would be the terrorist organizations with extremist religious ideologies. Think about the fact that Osama Bin Laden was once the leader of the most prominent extremist Islamist terrorist group and contrary to our expectations, his death had little to no affect on existence of extremist Islamist terrorist activities. As a matter of fact, in ideological brainwashing the death of a leader is considered an act of sacrifice for the greater good and leader is praised as martyrs.

"Most people do not really want freedom, because freedom involves responsibility, and most people are frightened of responsibility." – Sigmund Freud

When most people here the word terrorist group, they immediately think of ISIS and Al Qaeda, owing to the sheer horror these terrorists have put through the hearts and souls of American people. But violent terrorists can just as easily be motivated by extremist political views, originating from either side of the spectrum. However, the brainwashing tactics used by both these extremist groups to recruit and retain followers, remains the same. The extensive use of deliberate and carefully controlled brainwashing process has allowed the religious terrorist groups to recruit young people from across the West into the unstable Middle East. The shift of brainwashing tactics from a physical location for gathering and recruitment to the online high-definition propaganda videos to penetrate deep into the psyche of the impressionable and vulnerable youth has led to horrifying devastation in the society.

The first step of the brainwashing process is identification and analysis of the mental state and social circumstances of the prey. This step creates the foundation of the whole brainwashing process, as careful selection of the victim who is susceptible and vulnerable is essential. For example, people who have suffered death in their family are more likely to be enticed by the extremist groups like ISIS and detonate suicide bombs. These people had suffered mental trauma and their world as is had lost meaning so the brainwashers could easily step in and fill that void with their extremist views and murderous ideology.

Once the victim has been identified, either online or in person, the brainwasher will contact the victim in a very calm and friendly manner, giving the appearance of someone who has their world sorted out. It's like the victim is homeless and a celebrity walks in to befriend them, of course the victim is highly vulnerable. The brainwasher will then proceed to generate a rapport with the victim to create trust between them, by sharing real or made up stories about themselves that will resonate with the victim. They will start bonding over something as normal as sports or food and something truly intimate and emotional based on shared experiences. To further this "relationship", the brainwasher will offer favors and gifts to the victim to send a message that the victim can rely on them for any physical or emotional needs. The victim starts to develop a sense of indebtedness and gratitude towards their brainwasher, dissolving any initial resistance they might have experienced. For example, American troops that had been captured by the enemy, often report that they were offered American cigarettes and other American delicacies, so as to generate a sense of warmth in the troops and open them up to the brainwashing process.

Post the initial victim identification and rapport building stages, the brainwashing will present a utopian world to the victim, by gradually suggesting solutions to all the problems the victim has opened up about. The suggestions are made in a casual tone to avoid any sense of pressure that could be experienced by the victim. The utopian solution is always rooted in the ideologies or extremist views of the cult or the terrorist groups. The victim grows anxious and curious about all the possibilities laid out in front of them and craves more information and deeper understanding of the "solution". Once the brainwasher is satisfied with the extent of victim's curiosity and motivation, they are provided with the core ideologies which are absorbed by the victim as cold water on a hot day, natural and refreshing. The controversial ideas are always saved for the last and handed out only when the brainwasher deems the victim as positively primed and receptive to those ideas. For example, religious terrorist groups often convince their victim that the God loves them, as the first step. Once the victim develops a strong connection with the ideology and is driven to act in order to protect the very existence of the ideology, they are fed with ideas to kill those who the brainwasher pose a threat to the ideology. This is exactly how suicide bombers are created out of people who are pushed to the point of no return.

The dangerous consequences of Brainwashing are inevitable and long lasting. Of all the side effects of this process, loss of identity is insurmountable. Many cults and ideologies give their followers a new name up on their successful indoctrination. This opens a path for the individual to completely disconnect from their past identity and their old world. They experience this unhinged ability to follow their new whim given to them by their brainwasher. The victims turn into brainwashed zombies who are capable of antisocial behavior and commit heinous crimes like murder, rape and even suicide. They adopt this new lifestyle that they often feel blessed to have been introduced to and welcomed into.

Those few victims who have been rescued or managed to escape the brainwashing often develop PTSD (Post Traumatic Stress Disorder) and exhibit physical and psychological signs of damage, to the likes of of war veterans who have first hand witnessed the death of their fellow soldiers and friends during combat. The severity of this traumatic aftermath is evident in those cases where the rescued victim returns to their brainwasher of their own volition.

So the question arises, can you heal from brainwashing? The answer is Yes!

For ease of understanding, let's categorize the road to recovery from brainwashing and proactively protection yourself or your friends from being brainwashed, into three phases:

1. Recognizing the brainwashing tactics
2. Identifying those who have been brainwashed
3. Deprogramming and Healing

Recognizing the brainwashing tactics

A skilled brainwasher is adept at identifying the possible candidate for their dark tactics and people going through life condition such as loss of job, divorce, death of a loved one are highly vulnerable. The first step in any kind of healing is always acknowledgement. If you are able to recognize that you are being targeted for brainwashing, you are automatically positioning yourself to be able to holster your guards and protect yourself.

- Be mindful of people who may be trying to isolate you from the rest of the world. For example, cults often prevent their followers from contacting their friend and family.
- Watch for emotional attacks on your self esteem. Brainwashers often target their victim's mental and emotional vulnerabilities and damage them further to eventually build the victim back up with their own ideologies.
- Watch for people who are trying present you with a utopian world created on the basis of their own ideologies. The brainwasher provides the victim an alternative, more attractive reality as a one stop solution to all their problems.
- Watch for an "Us vs. Them" mentality being posed on you. This tactic is a hallmark of the charismatic cult leader.
- Recognize that the victims are often offered gifts and rewards as a gesture of inclusion and to create a feeling of indebtedness to their brainwasher.

- Watch for differences in the way of thinking of the potential victim. Brainwashers tend to use positive experiences to reward the victim for shared thoughts and ideas.
- Watch for any unusual behavioral patterns. For example, if an extremely social individual expresses low interest in attending social events for a long term, there might be a potential brainwasher behind it.

Identifying those have been brainwashed

- Look for signs of dependency and fanaticism. Brainwashing victims lose their identity to the brainwasher and rely heavily on the brainwasher to solve their problems.
- Look for extreme reactions to an otherwise normal incident or event. Brainwashing victims have a change in their beliefs, so they may act increasingly hostile to incidents that challenge or undermine their new beliefs.

- Brainwashing victims often disregard the consequences of their changed behavior and actions and blindly follow an individual to the point of obsession.

- Look for signs of withdrawal from social settings. Brainwashing victims are naturally drawn to those who share their views and isolate themselves from people with different opinions.

Deprogramming and Healing

In the past, deprogramming was carried out by keeping the victim locked up in a location to undo the mind control. They were given facts and information about the ideology of the group and its leader that was conveniently concealed from them by the brainwasher. The whole process was definitely traumatic but not very successful as victims often returned to the group. These days "exit counselling" is widely used. The victim is invited to speak with a specialist away from the brainwasher in a closed setting, who will eventually guide the victim through the brainwasher's deception.

Planned interventions are conducted by the victim's friends and families, trying to help the victim regain their reasoning and critical thinking. The victim is allowed control over the flow of the intervention and who they choose to discuss their thoughts and feelings with. The goal is to provide sufficient information and understanding to the victim, on how mind control works and how he had been victimized. By the end of the meeting, victim should learn the real intentions of their brainwasher and that they can choose to not return to the brainwashing group.

The final step is to seek therapeutic treatment to rinse out any remnants of the brainwashing. The victims are often unaware of the extent of the effects the mind control has had on their psyche and the therapist will aid this assessment. The aim of the therapist is to help the victim regain their lost identity and eventually to reintegrate into the society.

Remember, knowledge and education are crucial to undo mind control. The recognition that it exists is the first step. An extensive understanding of how mind control and brainwashing work and extreme vigilance, are the best ways to stop mind control from happening in the first place!

"Out of your vulnerabilities will come your strength." – Sigmund Freud

Chapter 7: Persuasion vs. Manipulation

Persuasion

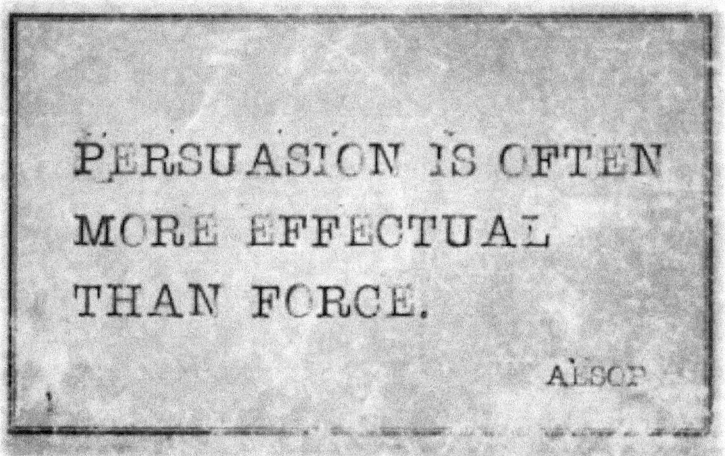

When you hear the word persuasion, what comes to your mind? Maybe the advertising jingles of a product urging you to buy a pizza from them, or maybe political campaign slogans trying to convince you to vote for a particular candidate, or maybe a pushy salesman trying to sell you a car. You are absolutely right if you think those are acts of persuasion! Politicians, news, mass media, legal proceedings and advertising can persuade you and influence your decision making. Most people like to think that they are immune to such influences. But then most of us own Nike sneakers, Ray Ban sunglasses or of course the new I-Phone. So advertising must have played a role in influencing your decision. Persuasion is constitutional within human communication and social interaction. When communicating, wittingly or unwittingly, people are always supporting and/or promoting certain ideas and behaviors over others. Therefore, persuasion is intrinsic to social interaction and not a matter of choice.

The study of attitudes and how to change them can also be referred to as Persuasion. Most of the things that involve molding attitudes that shape our world, involve persuasion. It is through persuasion that positive changes can be brought to the society. It is persuasion that convinces motorists to drive sober and buckle up. It is persuasion that helps end wars and forge peace between nations. According to

Professor of Communication at Cleveland Stat University, Richard Perloff, defined Persuasion as "A symbolic process in which communicators try to convince other people to change their attitudes or behaviors regarding an issue through the transmission of a message in an atmosphere of free choice". The main components of Persuasion are:

- Persuasion incorporates symbols, verbal and non verbal, to change attitudes. For example, images like Nike Swoosh or Adidas Three Stripes; words like freedom and justice; non verbal signs like Holy Cross or Star of David.

- Persuasion involves a conscious and thoughtful attempt to influence another person. The persuader is always aware of the potential susceptibility of the person to accept change.

- Persuasion is a voluntary act of changing our own attitude or behavior.

- Persuasion is completely driven by the science of communication and requires a relay of verbal or non verbal message to the persuaded.

- Persuasion of the self is at the heart of the art of Persuasion. People must always be free to decide if and how they want to change their attitude and behavior.

In 1980, Gerald Miller, suggested that communications can exert different persuasive effects, namely:

- *Shaping* - For example, the Nike ad campaign featuring Michael Jordan connecting the Nike Swoosh with the idea of superhuman athleticism.
- *Reinforcing* - For example, health experts make public statements to bolster the people's continuing resolve to abstain from excessive drinking.
- *Changing* – For example, the civil rights campaigns increased dialogue between Blacks and Whites and brought about radical changes in the

Perhaps the foremost rule of good persuasion is stating suggestions using value-free verbiage. Persuasive is a positive act made in an attempt to alter people's opinion. For example, if you were visiting abroad and walked into a restaurant. You are very hungry but confused as to what you should order. As you are looking through the menu you come across a section labelled "Most Popular Dishes" or "Specialties", you are very likely to order a dish from that section.

Aristotle, the world renowned Greek philosopher, is credited to have laid the foundation of the art of Persuasion. Aristotle claimed that *"Of the modes of persuasion furnished by the spoken word there are three kinds. The first kind depends on the personal character of the speaker [ethos]; the second on putting the audience into a certain frame of mind [pathos]; the third on the proof, or apparent proof, provided by the words of the speech itself [logos].*

Persuasion is achieved by the speaker's personal character when the speech is so spoken as to make us think him credible."

Ethos (Character)

Aristotle suggested three major contributing factors to Ethos: "good moral character (arête); goodwill (eunoia); and good sense (phronesis)". The persuader must be able to build credibility and rapport with their audience. The word "Ethics" is in fact derived from "Ethos". Ethos, the ethical appeal, refers to the author's character and credibility as perceived by the audience. For instance, if you were sick and your doctor recommended treatment A and your close friend who has no medical background recommended treatment B, you will definitely choose treatment A since it was recommended by someone you think has credibility in that field. But odds are you are more likely to take a recommendation on new movies from your friend than your doctor.

Pathos (Emotion/Empathy)

Widely used colloquial term such as apathy, sympathy, pathetic and of course empathy is derived from "Pathos". Pathos can be defined as an act of using shared stories and experiences to invoke emotions in the audience. In Greek language, Pathos means suffering and experience. This method can be used to draw pity or incite anger in the audience, to prompt them into action.

Aristotle suggested these mutually exclusive positive and negative emotions, that can be used by the persuader to build empathy with their audience: "Anger and Calmness; Envy and Emulation; Enmity and Friendship; Fear and Confidence; Kindness and Unkindness; Pity and Indignation; Shame and Shamelessness".

The powerful tool of Pathos, allows the persuader to stir desired emotions in the audience, by creating a bond and building empathy. The power of Empathy must not be undermined as human emotions always trump reasoning. Look at our history, the most influential political leaders were able to win their arguments by emotionally and empathetically persuading their audiences. For example, Martin Luther King, Jr's "I have a dream" speech, was able to invoke empathy for Black community in the White community and had a revolutionary effect in shaping the modern America.

The art of building Empathy

By building empathy, audience is more receptive to their persuader's message. To be able to successfully persuade your audience, you must be able to understand the pre-disposed emotions of your audience. Take your audience's state of mind in consideration and assess why they feel that way and to whom those emotions are directed at. Your ability to build empathy and emotional connection with your audience, in turn, builds your Ethos (character and credibility) with the audience.

Here are few ways to help you build empathy with your audience:

- We are all human! - If you can easily blend in with your audience and make them see you as a part of their own "community", people will inevitably connect with you emotionally.
- Be authentic – Nobody wants to be manipulated. If your audience suspects that you have ulterior motives and are not genuinely "one of them", you will lose all your credibility instantly.
- Structure your statements to resonate with the audience. Every topic has multiple aspects and underlying perspectives to it. The key is to find what would work with your audience. For

example, there might be speakers headlining to talk about preservation of wildlife. One might state "You can make a difference - Wildlife needs our help!" and other might state "Symposium on wildlife preservation". I know which speaker I will be listening to.

- Narrate a story – Human psyche is hardwired to exhibit emotional responses to stories. Stories tend to be more memorable and inspire action. Personal stories have huge impact in building empathy but you could also share stories of someone you know or even fables. The act of story telling will give an impression to your audience that you have an understanding of the underlying emotion and your take on it.

- Metaphorical speech – Similar to story telling, metaphors tend to be more memorable and make your speech intriguing. In words of Aristotle, metaphors give charm, clearness and distinction to your speech like no other. For example, MLK's use of banking metaphor in his "I have a dream speech", was met with thunderous applause. MLK said *"Instead of honoring this sacred obligation, America has given the Negro people a bad check, a check which has come back marked "insufficient funds." But we refuse to believe that the bank of justice is bankrupt. We refuse to believe that there are insufficient funds in the great vaults of opportunity of this nation. And so, we've come to cash this check, a check that will give us upon demand the riches of freedom and the security of justice."*

- Use visual aids – Remember "A picture is worth a thousand words"! Using powerful images will incite emotions and help build empathy with the audience. For example, recently a picture of a Syrian boy bruised and helpless went viral, because it created a wave of empathy for the survivors of the ongoing Syrian war.

- Delivery of speech – It goes without saying that your tone and volume of the speech must befit your audience.

- Power of words – The English language has a bountiful of synonyms for everyday terms, providing a spectrum of intensity for the same emotion. For example, pain and agony; hungry and starving or sad and devastated. Have a thesaurus handy and use appropriate words.

Logos (Logic/Reasoning)

The word "logic" is, you guessed it, derived from Logos. In Greek language, Logos literally means "word". Logos refers to the act of appealing to the mind of your audience, using logic or reason. The effective persuader recognizes that using Logos alone, without Pathos and Ethos, poses them with a risk of losing their audience. With this type of persuasion, only facts and statistics can be employed in altering the attitude and behavior of the audience. There is no room for lies and deception. The appeal to reason is a measured and careful representation of facts and information in a logical way. The theory of logic can be categorized into two: Deductive reasoning and Inductive reasoning.

Deductive Reasoning – It's based on the assumption that if the premise is true, the conclusion would be true as well. For example, if the assumption is children love ice cream and you are presented with premise that Jack is a child. You can safely conclude that Jack loves ice cream.

Inductive Reasoning – As expected, Inductive reasoning is reverse engineering the premise from conclusion. Therefore, even if the premise is true, the conclusion may be false. For example, if the premise is 25% of American athletes like to read, the conclusion that 25% of American population likes to read may or may not be true.

Manipulation

Psychological Manipulation can be defined as a way to influence people's emotions, attitudes or behaviors which is neither rational persuasion nor coercion. The term manipulation is inherently thought of as negative and involving an element of moral deprecation. Human beings are inherently gregarious which makes them influence one another all the time. Consider, the influence your older sibling had on you growing up. That is a classic example of "healthy social influence" and must not be confused with the dark act of manipulation. In Psychological Manipulation, the goal of the manipulator is always to influence their victim into fulfilling their own desires.

People often confuse "manipulation" with "influencing" but they are poles apart in practice. Starting with the intent and motive of the person; an influencer is often looking for your best interest and approaches you with advice on how to make a decision better; but a manipulator has the mindset of how can I control your thoughts and emotions to get a better decision from you for myself. Thus, understanding the motive behind any such behavior plays a pivotal role in deciding whether it is a situation of "influencing", "manipulation" or even Covert Emotional Manipulation.

Covert Emotional Manipulation

The most widespread form of manifestation of Dark Psychology in today's world, which after reading this book you might agree with is Covert Emotional Manipulation (CEM). Now you are probably thinking is that different from Emotional Manipulation and if so, how. The answer is

Emotional Manipulation occurs within the realms of your consciousness so you are aware that someone is trying to appeal to a more generous side of you to get what they want. Think about the time when your parents wanted you to visit them for the summer but you had a different probably more exciting summer plans with your friends or a special someone and your parents insisted you visit them instead or take some extra time off to make the visit. You tried to convince them that you would visit for Thanksgiving and your calendar is booked solid and they might have retorted with statements like "we are old and we wouldn't be around for so long, you need to make us your priority" or "we haven't seen you in forever and we miss you, come over to visit your loving parents". During this conversation you are completely aware that your parents are attempting to change how you feel about your summer plans in their favor. This is a classic and harmless case of Emotional Manipulation. On the other hand, Covert Emotional Manipulation is carried out by individuals who are trying to gain influence over your thought process and feelings, with the means of subtle underhanded tactics that go undetected by the person being manipulated.

By definition Covert Emotional Manipulation goes undetected and leaves you acting like a pawn in the hands of the manipulator, which makes this a manifestation of Dark Psychology. The dictionary definition of the word covert is "not openly shown or engaged in", therefore, it presents a stark difference from all other Emotional Manipulation techniques. The victims of Covert Emotional Manipulation are unable to understand the intent or motivation of the manipulator and the way they are being manipulation and even just the fact that they are being manipulated. Think of Covert Emotional Manipulation as a bomber with impeccable stealth, one that can tip toe in your subconscious without being detected, leaving you with no defense what so ever. Our emotions primarily dictate all other aspects of our personality and thus they also dictate our reality. Someone attempting to manipulate your emotions is equivalent to them cutting open your jugular vein making you lose control over yourself and your reality.

In this book, we have also covered some prominent and dark types of Manipulation, namely, Machiavellianism and Brainwashing in detail. But the are many more types of Psychological Manipulation in our society. Let's have a brief look at some of the more frequently observed forms of dark manipulation.

Gaslighting

The tactic used by manipulators aimed at making their victim doubt their own thoughts and feelings is called Gaslighting. This term is often used by mental health professionals to describe the manipulative behavior to convince the victim into thinking their thoughts and feelings are off base and not in alignment with the situation at hand.

Passive-Aggressive behavior

Manipulators can adopt this duplicitous behavior to criticize, change or intervene the behavior of their victim without making direct requests or aggressive gestures. Some of these traits include: sulking or giving the silent treatment, portraying themselves as a victim or intentionally cryptic speech.

Withholding information

There is no such thing as a white lie but manipulators often provide selective information to their victim, so as to guide them into their web of deception.

Isolation

Dark manipulator is always aiming to gain control and authority on their victim. In order to succeed they will create an increasingly isolated environment for their victim and prevent them from contacting their friends and family.

The many differences between Persuasion and Manipulation

1. Motive/Intent

As we have established people with active dark psychological traits including manipulators, aim to establish control and authority on their prey and exploit their victims to serve their own interests. On the other hand, persuaders are concerned about the well being of their audience and attempt to convince them to change their attitude or behavior in a free environment.

2. Method of Delivery

Manipulators create an inviting environment for their victim, who is often an unwilling prey and primed emotionally and psychologically to act in ways that benefit their predators and threatens their own health or well-being. Whereas, persuaders only hope that their audience will respond to their influence and the suggestions. Ultimately the individual is free to decide whether or not they want to accept the suggestions made by their persuader and alter their thoughts, feelings and/or behaviors.

3. Impact on the social interaction

Dark manipulators will always aim to isolate their prey from the rest of the world and prevent any contact from their loved ones. The victim of dark manipulation like brainwashing, develop extreme views and may commit heinous acts of antisocial behavior. Unlike manipulation, acts of persuasion are never lethal for the audience and the society. It could be as harmless as your brother's admiration for Nike shoes leading you to buy a pair of your own or the ads from McDonalds inviting you to enjoy a quick meal with your family.

4. Final outcome

Persuasion usually result in one of these three possible scenarios: Benefit to both the persuaded and the persuader, commonly known as a win-win situation; Benefit only to the persuaded; Benefit to the persuaded and a third party. However, dark manipulation always has a singular benefactor that is the manipulator. The manipulated individual is at grave disadvantage and will act against their own self interest.

"The systematic use of misleading influence tactics ultimately becomes a psychologically and financially self-damaging process." – Robert Cialdini

To drive this difference home, let's consider this example. Brian is on a budget and walks in the store looking to buy a new Smart TV. He is greeted by Adam, who then proceeds to show him all the Smart TVs available in the store. Adam explains to Brian all the unique features of different models and says "So and so Samsung model is little over your budget but it is the hottest product on the market with the best audio and video quality and is worth going over your budget". Now, If Adam truly believes in his recommended TV model and has the best interest at heart for his customer. That's definitely act of Persuasion. On the other hand, if it so happens that Adam's recommended is not really worth its high price but that sale would make him extra commission, so he convinced Brian into buying a bad product at high cost. That's manipulation!

Now that you have an understanding of Dark Psychology of manipulation, I offer you few scenarios in which dark manipulation can take place so you are armed to be able to detect it and protect yourself.

1. Disengage. If someone is trying to get on your good side and then ask for an overwhelming favor, simply decline politely and move on with the conversation.

2. Don't second guess yourself. Manipulators will try to convince you that your thoughts and

behaviors are off base. Take a moment and assess whether the suggestion made by the person will benefit them or yourself and act accordingly.

3. Call them out. If you have successfully spotted the manipulation, don't be afraid to address the situation in a logical, respectful manner. Use of accusatory tone with a friend will just ruin your friendship so decide the sentence based on the crime.

4. Don't let them digress when you have spotted the manipulation. The manipulator and especially covert emotionally manipulator will not be prepared to get caught and will try to muddle the situation so as to minimize the harm.

5. If you are being probed to give out personal information, don't play in the hands of the manipulator. The manipulator is attempting to baseline your thought process and behavior to evaluate your strengths and pounce on your weaknesses.

6. Ask for details. Remember manipulators seek to withhold information from you so as to paint their own version of reality for you. If you feel you are being presented with a partial view of the situation, grill them for more information and make sound decisions.

7. Beware of exaggeration. Some manipulators can adopt an opposite approach and bombard you with additional and often vague details about the situation, in order to confuse you or even mentally exhaust you to cave in and accept the manipulation.

8. Verify the facts. Lying and deception come naturally to the manipulator. They will often manipulate facts or present false information to pressure you into making a hasty decision. Do not fall for the lies and "Google" your way to safety!

9. Scrutinize the bureaucracy. Certain manipulators may try to intimidate you with paperwork, procedures and laws to exert their power and authority. Don't undermine

yourself and read through the paperwork and research the procedure and laws. Make well informed decisions

10.   Don't be intimidated by their aggressive behavior. Some manipulators will play out front and center. They will raise their voice or display negative emotions with strong body language, to make you submit to their coercion. Stay strong and firm!

11. Take your time. I cannot emphasize this enough. If someone is rushing you into making a decision, by creating false deadlines or conveying a sense of urgency for your benefit, be sure to take control, step back and make a well informed decision.

12. See through those negative remarks and criticism. Skilled dark manipulators can resort to humor or sarcasm to make you feel inferior and insecure. They are trying to establish superiority over you by constantly marginalizing and ridiculing you. Don't let

them get to you and reassure yourself that you are full of potential.

13. Don't take on responsibilities willy-nilly. The manipulator can use the classic "playing dumb" tactic to make you take on their own workload. For example, if a coworker is pretending they don't understand what you expect of them, knowing full well the project deadline is looming. You should call out their bluff and not let them get away with no work.

14. Don't give them leverage over you. If the manipulator is giving you the "silent treatment", don't get agitated and hold your ground. They are attempting to make you second guess yourself and asset power over you.

15. Get a grip on your soft side. The manipulator will always seek to take advantage of you and appeal to your soft spot. They will attempt to exploit your emotional weaknesses and vulnerabilities and use them as ammunitions against you.

16. Patience is a virtue! If you can control your anxiety and excitement, you are always in a better position to make rational decisions.

17. Self awareness. Knowing and acknowledging your strengths and weakness will help you design your defenses accordingly. When the manipulator is trying to strike a nerve to get an extreme reaction out of you and then subsequently guilt you into making decisions that will only help them, use your mental strength to overcome the manipulation.

18. Develop healthy coping mechanisms. We all go through ups and downs in life but a lot of people look to alcohol and overeating to distress. Remember there are no answers at the bottom of that bottle and carb coma will eventually lead to diseases.

19. Be easy on yourself. You are your own best friend! There is always a dawn after the dusk. We all cannot be good at just everything we ever decide to do. Learn you lesson and give

yourself a break. Practice meditation to silence your mind and find inner peace.

20.   Avoid being overly dependent on others. It's totally acceptable to seek help but if you develop chronic dependencies on others to resolve your problems, you will begin to undermine yourself and lose the confidence you need to protect yourself from the dark manipulator.

21. Give yourself pep talk every now and then. You can restore your metal health and well-being by saying uplifting affirmations to yourself. Positivity is the foundation of good mental health.

Chapter 8: General FAQs

Q1.   What is the difference between Dark Psychology and dark psychological traits?

A.   Dark Psychology is the study of innate human behavioral patterns as it relates to the psychological nature of people to victimize other humans and living creatures. Understanding the inherent thoughts, feelings and perceptions of humans that leads to human predatory behavior is at the heart of Dark Psychology studies. On the other hand, dark psychological traits refer to the personality traits exhibited by people that are inherently immoral, antisocial and harmful to other people. Some dark personality traits that we have covered in detail in this book are Narcissism, Machiavellianism and Psychopathy.

Q2.   What is Dark Continuum and how does it manifest in our world?

A.   The Dark Continuum is a spectrum within which all criminal, sadistic and violent behaviors of the human psyche fall, including thoughts, feelings and actions committed against and/or experienced by individuals. The Dark Continuum can range from severe to mild manifestation and from purpose driven to purposeless. The physical manifestation of Dark Psychology more often than not fall to the right of the Dark Continuum with high severity. On the other hand, the psychological manifestations of Dark Psychology lie to the left of the Dark Continuum, but could potentially be just as destructive as the physical manifestations. Rather than acting as a scale of severity, ranging from bad to worse, Dark Continuum provides a classification of victimization considering the thoughts and actions perpetrated.

Q3.   How do you define the Dark Triad and its underlying dark personality traits?

A.   The concept of the Dark Triad is relatively new to psychology and paramount to the understanding of Dark Psychology. The term the Dark Triad can be defined as an unholy trinity of the three most offensive yet non-pathological personality variables: Narcissism, Psychopathy and Machiavellianism.

Narcissism – A mental health condition marked by elevated and self detrimental involvement, deep need for excessive attention and admiration and a lack of empathy.

Machiavellianism – Refers to predisposition of conniving and deceptive traits in individuals that are also inherently master manipulators.

Psychopathy – Can be defined as a mental disorder, when an individual manifests antisocial behaviors, shows no signs of empathy and remorse, expresses extreme egocentricity, lacks the ability to establish meaningful personal relationships masked with superficial charm and impulsivity.

Q4.   Can Neuro-Linguistic Programming (NLP) be used on anyone and how can I know if someone is using NLP on me?

A.   Yes, NLP can be used on just about anyone wittingly or unwittingly. NLP therapy or training can be delivered in the form of language and sensory based interventions, using behavior modification techniques customized for individuals to better their social communication and improved confidence and self awareness. If you ever feel like you have involuntarily acted in ways you cannot explain or control, then you may have been programmed for that reaction. Be aware of people who seem to always touch your back or arm during conversations or are mirroring your body language to the point of abnormality.

Q5.   Where can I learn NLP and can I ethically use it on my friends and family?

A.   There are plenty of NLP trainers and workshops being offered all over the world. Just Google to find one with sufficient credibility and that meets your need. Be mindful of false publicity and of course, spams.

If your intention to use NLP on friends and family is pure and will not cause any psychological and physical harm to the person then you will be able to use NLP on them ethically. Don't get carried away with your new power!

Q6.   Someone I know is exhibiting unusually different thoughts and feelings to an otherwise normal situation. What can I do to help them?

A.   A lot of people who are victims of undetected mind control or worse, brainwashing experience altered thoughts and feelings at the beginning. The dark manifestation of undetected mind control prevents the victim from recognizing the attack and control on their psyche. However, in brainwashing, the victim knows that the aggressor is an enemy but is not able to release themselves from the entanglements of the aggressor. In either case, you can help your friend by having an open conversation about their altered thoughts and behaviors and subsequently empowering them to recognize their predator and protect themselves from further harm.

Q7.   Are the various tests mentioned in this book available online for self assessment and how reliable are they?

A.   Yes, most of the tests discussed in this book such as: Dirty Dozens scale, The Mach-IV test and Hare PCL-R test, are easily available online for self assessment but they can only present you with a possibility of any dark psychological traits that might be a part of your personality. A true and valid diagnosis can only be made by a certified and licenses psychological therapist.

Q8.   What is the difference between counselling

and psychotherapy?

A.   These two terms are often used interchangeably but there is a slight and distinctive difference between psychotherapy and counselling. "Psychotherapy is often treatment based in response to a diagnosable mental health issue such as depression, bi-polar disorder, attention deficit hyperactivity disorder, adjustment disorder, etc. It is often in-depth and used in conjunction with psychotropic medication, but not necessarily. Counselling tends to be wellness oriented, providing increased insight and learning how to effectively overcome problems and challenges."

Q9.   When should I visit a mental health professional and what can I expect during my first visit?

A.   Finding the right mental health professional and the right approach to therapy is as important as finding the right medical doctor. Whether you are planning to see a psychologist or a psychiatrist or another type of mental health professional, you should start with a phone call to the professional. Ask about the professional's approach to dealing with mental issues and how he or she generally works with clients. Ask about whether or not he or she accepts insurance and how payments are handled. You might describe your reason for wanting to make an appointment and ask if he or she is experienced in dealing with such issues. If you are comfortable talking with him or her, the next step is to make an appointment.

At your first office visit, the mental health professional will want to talk with you about why you think you need to come to therapy. He or she will want to know about what your symptoms are, how long you've had them and what, if anything, you've done about them in the past. He or she will probably ask you about your family and your work as well as what you do to relax. This initial conversation is important in developing the appropriate approach to treatment. Before you leave the office, the mental health professional should describe to you the plan for treatment and give you an opportunity to ask any questions you might have.

It will likely take several weeks before you become fully comfortable with your therapy. If you still aren't feeling comfortable after two or three visits, let the mental health professional know and explain why you feel that way. The two of you need to work together as a team in order to get the most out of your treatment.

Conclusion

Thank you for making it through to the end of *Dark Psychology Secrets: The Ultimate Guide to Improve Social Influence, Analyze People Using NLP & Body Language Techniques, including tips for Mind Control, Persuasion & Manipulation*, let's hope it was informative and able to provide you with all of the tools you need to achieve your goals whatever they may be.

The next step is to make the best use of your new found wisdom of Dark Psychology and protect yourself and your loved ones from being a victim at the hands of predators using their Dark Psychology to their own advantage. Take a step back and reassess the negative influences in your life. You have now armed yourself to fight them back with your knowledge and understanding of the Dark Psychology and its various modes of manifestation. You have also learned how NLP can help you transform your weaknesses and insecurities into positive affirmations and increasing confidence. Mastering the art of persuasion will allow you to help your loved ones into making better life decisions and with your renewed understanding of the difference between persuasion and dark manipulation, you can easily identify your friends from your enemies. Remember with great power, comes get responsibility. So exercise caution while using your new psychological powers.

We really hope you enjoyed this guide, customer satisfaction for us is very important.
If you found this book useful in any way, a review on Amazon is always appreciated! ☺

Ehy, one more thing:
Don't miss the other 2 books of the series called "Mental Toughness by Daniel Travis" and "Emotional Intelligence 2.0 by Daniel Travis"

Inside Mental Toughness you will find:

- What is Mindset and why it is important?

- How to develop a Positive, Strong Mindset

- How to awaken your Life for Success?

- Productivity Secrets to dominate.

- ... and much, much more!

Inside Emotional Intelligence 2.0 you will find:

- What is emotional intelligence and why it is important?

- The History of emotional intelligence

- Cognitive Behavioral Therapy and its use in emotional intelligence

- You will learn how to increase your emotional intelligence.

- You will learn techniques to gain more self-awareness, self-confidence and self-discipline.

- ... and much, much more!

THANK YOU

www.ingramcontent.com/pod-product-compliance
Lightning Source LLC
Chambersburg PA
CBHW061755250726
48657CB00001B/139